FAVORITE BRAND NAME RECIPES™

Most Requested RECIPES

Publications International, Ltd.

Pictured on the front cover: *(clockwise from top left)*: Easy Fried Rice *(page 71)*, Chicken Kabobs with Thai Dipping Sauce *(page 31)*, Milk Chocolate Florentine Cookies *(page 203)*, and Korean Soft Tacos *(page 158)*.

Pictured on the back cover *(left to right)*: Creamy Vegetable Lasagna *(page 166)*, Buffalo Chicken Wings *(page 32)*, and HERSHEY'S® HUGS® & KISSES® Candies Chocolate Cake *(page 216)*.

ISBN-13: 978-1-68022-033-9

Library of Congress Control Number: 201590087

Manufactured in China.

8 7 6 5 4 3 2 1

Microwave Cooking: Microwave ovens vary in wattage. Use the cooking times as guidelines and check for doneness before adding more time.

Preparation/Cooking Times: Preparation times are based on the approximate amount of time required to assemble the recipe before cooking, baking, chilling or serving. These times include preparation steps such as measuring, chopping and mixing. The fact that some preparations and cooking can be done simultaneously is taken into account. Preparation of optional ingredients and serving suggestions is not included.

Contents

Breakfast & Brunch

TOLL HOUSE® Mini Morsel Pancakes

2½ cups all-purpose flour

1 cup (6 ounces) NESTLÉ® TOLL HOUSE® Semi-Sweet Chocolate Mini Morsels

1 tablespoon baking powder

½ teaspoon salt

1¾ cups milk

2 large eggs

⅓ cup vegetable oil

⅓ cup packed brown sugar

Powdered sugar

Fresh sliced strawberries (optional)

Maple syrup

Prep Time: 8 minutes
Cooking Time: 4 minutes

COMBINE flour, morsels, baking powder and salt in large bowl. Combine milk, eggs, vegetable oil and brown sugar in medium bowl; add to flour mixture. Stir just until moistened (batter may be lumpy).

HEAT griddle or skillet over medium heat; brush lightly with vegetable oil. Pour ¼ *cup* of batter onto hot griddle; cook until bubbles begin to burst. Turn; continue to cook for about 1 minute longer or until golden. Repeat with *remaining* batter.

SPRINKLE with powdered sugar; top with strawberries. Serve with maple syrup.

Makes about 18 pancakes

Spinach Quiche

1 tablespoon vegetable oil

½ onion, chopped

2 tablespoons POLANER®
Chopped Garlic

1 bunch spinach, washed,
trimmed, chopped*

4 large eggs

½ cup milk

⅓ cup CREAM OF WHEAT®
Hot Cereal (Instant,
1-minute, 2½-minute or
10-minute cook time),
uncooked

½ teaspoon salt

½ teaspoon ground black
pepper

1½ cups shredded sharp
Cheddar, colby or
Monterey Jack cheese

*Or substitute 1 (10-ounce) package frozen
chopped spinach, thawed, squeezed dry.

Prep Time: 15 minutes
Start to Finish Time: 55 minutes

1. Preheat oven to 375°F. Coat 10-inch pie pan with nonstick cooking spray.

2. Heat oil in large skillet over medium-high heat. Add onion and garlic; cook and stir 8 minutes or until soft. Add spinach. Cook and stir until spinach is wilted (if using frozen spinach, cook until heated through). Remove from heat and let cool slightly.

3. Combine eggs, milk, Cream of Wheat, salt and pepper in large bowl; mix well. Stir in spinach mixture and cheese. Pour into prepared pan. Bake 30 minutes or until just firm in center and lightly browned along the edges. Cool 10 minutes before serving.

Makes 6 servings

TIP

Because you don't need a crust for this quick-to-fix, tasty egg-and-cheese pie, you can use this recipe as a starting point for other types of quiche. Substitute any greens for the spinach, and use almost any combination of cheeses for a different flavor. For extra flair, stir in chopped fresh herbs. The quiche is best hot out of the oven, but can be served cold or at room temperature.

Blueberry Bundt Cake

- 3 cups all-purpose flour
- 1 tablespoon baking powder
- ½ teaspoon salt
- ¼ teaspoon baking soda
- 1 cup COUNTRY CROCK® Calcium plus Vitamin D or COUNTRY CROCK® Spread
- 2¼ cups granulated sugar, divided
- 4 large eggs
- 2½ teaspoons vanilla extract, divided
- 1 cup sour cream
- 2 cups fresh blueberries, rinsed and dried and tossed with 1 tablespoon all-purpose flour
- 1½ cups confectioners sugar
- 1½ to 2 tablespoons fresh lemon juice
- 1 teaspoon grated lemon peel

Prep Time: 15 minutes
Cook Time: 55 minutes

1. Preheat oven to 350°F. Generously grease and flour 10-inch bundt pan; set aside.

2. Combine 3 cups flour, baking powder, salt and baking soda in medium bowl with wire whisk; set aside.

3. Beat COUNTRY CROCK® Calcium plus Vitamin D with 2 cups granulated sugar in large bowl with electric mixer until light and fluffy, about 5 minutes. Add eggs, one at a time, beating well after each addition. Beat in 2 teaspoons vanilla, scraping sides occasionally. Alternately beat in flour mixture and sour cream on low speed, just until blended, beginning and ending with flour mixture.

4. Combine remaining ¼ cup granulated sugar with blueberries. Gently fold blueberry mixture into cake batter. Spoon batter into prepared pan.

5. Bake 55 minutes or until toothpick inserted in center comes out clean. Cool on wire rack 15 minutes. Remove cake from pan and cool completely.

6. For glaze, blend confectioners sugar, lemon juice, lemon peel and remaining ½ teaspoon vanilla in medium bowl; drizzle over cake.

Makes 12 servings

Breakfast Burritos

½ **pound (8 ounces) ground sausage**

1 **large potato, peeled and grated**

2 **(8-inch) ORTEGA® Flour Soft Tortillas**

4 **eggs**

1 **can (4 ounces) ORTEGA® Fire-Roasted Diced Green Chiles**

ORTEGA® Salsa, any variety, divided

1 **large tomato, diced**

½ **cup (2 ounces) shredded Cheddar cheese**

Salt and black pepper, to taste

Prep Time: 15 minutes
Start to Finish Time: 25 minutes

COOK sausage in skillet; add potatoes. Cook until brown. Drain fat.

WARM tortillas according to package directions. Cook and scramble eggs.

DIVIDE eggs, sausage mixture, chiles, salsa, tomato and cheese evenly among tortillas.

SEASON to taste with salt and pepper.

FOLD tortillas and serve immediately. Top with additional salsa, if desired.

Makes 2 servings

Berry Smoothie

1 ripe, medium DOLE®
   Banana, peeled

1 can (6 ounces) or ¾ cup
   DOLE® Pineapple Juice

1 carton (6 ounces)
   blueberry or mixed
   berries yogurt

1 cup DOLE® Frozen
   Blueberries, partially
   thawed

Prep Time: 5 minutes

COMBINE banana, pineapple juice, yogurt and blueberries in blender or food processor container. Cover; blend until smooth.

Makes 3 servings

Mixed Fruit Smoothies

1 **peeled and frozen banana**

1 **cup orange juice**

1 **cup fat-free plain yogurt**

1 **cup frozen strawberries or raspberries**

¼ **cup EQUAL® SPOONFUL***

*May substitute 6 packets EQUAL® sweetener.

• Peel and cut banana into large chunks. Place in plastic freezer bag; seal and freeze at least 5 to 6 hours or overnight.

• Place all ingredients in blender or food processor. Blend until smooth.

Makes 2 servings

Breakfast Bake

1 **pound ground pork sausage**

1 **teaspoon Italian seasoning**

½ **teaspoon salt**

6 **eggs**

2 **cups milk**

½ **cup CREAM OF WHEAT® Hot Cereal (Instant, 1-minute, 2½-minute or 10-minute cook time), uncooked**

1 **teaspoon TRAPPEY'S® Red Devil™ Cayenne Pepper Sauce**

4 **cups cubed bread stuffing (potato bread recommended)**

2 **cups Cheddar cheese, shredded**

Prep Time: 30 minutes
Start to Finish Time:
4 to 12 hours soaking, 45 minutes baking

1. Brown sausage in skillet, pressing with fork or spatula to crumble as it cooks. Sprinkle on Italian seasoning and salt; set aside.

2. Combine eggs, milk, Cream of Wheat and pepper sauce in large mixing bowl; mix well. Add cooked sausage and bread stuffing; toss to combine. Pour mixture into 13×9-inch casserole pan; cover. Refrigerate at least 4 hours or overnight.

3. Preheat oven to 350°F. Remove cover and sprinkle cheese over casserole. Cover pan with aluminum foil; bake 30 minutes. Remove foil; bake 15 minutes longer. Serve warm.

Makes 8 servings

Serving Suggestion: Serve this dish with a salad and some fresh fruit on holiday mornings or for a special brunch.

Baked Cherry-Almond Oatmeal

2¼ cups QUAKER® Oats (quick or old fashioned, uncooked)

½ cup firmly packed brown sugar

½ teaspoon salt

3 cups reduced-fat (2%) milk

3 eggs, lightly beaten

1 tablespoon melted butter (optional)

1 teaspoon vanilla

¼ to ½ teaspoon almond extract

¾ cup dried cherries

½ cup toasted sliced almonds

Low-fat vanilla yogurt

1. Heat oven to 350°F. Spray 8 (6-ounce) custard cups or ramekins with nonstick cooking spray; arrange on rimmed baking sheet.

2. Combine oats, brown sugar and salt in large bowl; mix well. Whisk together milk, eggs, butter, if desired, vanilla and almond extract in medium bowl. Add to dry ingredients; mix until well blended. Spoon into cups. Stir cherries into each cup, dividing evenly; sprinkle evenly with almonds.

3. Bake until knife inserted near center comes out clean, about 23 to 26 minutes for quick oats, 25 to 30 minutes for old fashioned oats. (Centers will not be completely set.) Cool 10 minutes. To serve, top with yogurt.

Makes 8 servings

Variations: Substitute dried cranberries, blueberries or chopped dried apricots for dried cherries.

To bake in 8-inch square baking pan, spray pan with nonstick cooking spray. Prepare oatmeal as directed. Pour into pan, stir in cherries and sprinkle with almonds. Bake until knife inserted near center comes out clean, about 30 to 35 minutes.

COOK'S TIP

To toast almonds, spread in single layer on cookie sheet. Bake at 350°F about 6 to 8 minutes or until lightly browned and fragrant, stirring occasionally. Cool before using. Or, spread in single layer on microwave-safe plate. Microwave on HIGH (100% power) 1 minute; stir. Continue to microwave on HIGH, checking every 30 seconds, until nuts are fragrant and brown. Cool before using.

Cinnamon Walnut Coffee Cake

¾ cup chopped walnuts

1 teaspoon ground cinnamon

1¼ cups sugar

1 cup (2 sticks) butter, softened

2 eggs

1 cup sour cream

1⅓ cups all-purpose flour

⅓ cup CREAM OF WHEAT® Cinnamon Swirl Instant Hot Cereal, uncooked

1½ teaspoons baking powder

½ teaspoon baking soda

1 teaspoon vanilla extract

Prep Time: 15 minutes
Start to Finish Time: 1 hour

1. Coat Bundt® pan with nonstick cooking spray. Sprinkle lightly with flour; shake out any excess. Combine walnuts and cinnamon in small bowl; set aside.

2. Cream sugar, butter and eggs in mixing bowl with electric mixer at medium speed. Add sour cream; blend well. Add flour, Cream of Wheat, baking powder and baking soda; mix well. Stir in vanilla. Sprinkle half of walnut mixture into bottom of prepared Bundt pan. Evenly spread half of batter over mixture. Sprinkle remaining walnut mixture over batter. Top with remaining batter, spreading evenly in Bundt pan.

3. Set oven to 350°F (do not preheat); place Bundt pan in cold oven. Bake 45 minutes or until toothpick inserted into center comes out clean. Remove from oven; let stand 5 minutes. Place serving plate over Bundt pan and turn pan over carefully onto plate; remove pan. Serve cake warm or cool.

Makes 12 to 16 servings

TIP

If you do not have a Bundt® pan, you can bake this cake in regular square or round cake pans. Divide the batter between two 8- or 9-inch pans, and sprinkle each with one-half of walnut mixture. Bake 25 to 30 minutes.

Soy Milk Smoothie

3 cups plain or vanilla soy milk

1 banana, peeled and frozen

1 cup frozen strawberries or raspberries

1 teaspoon vanilla or almond extract

⅓ cup EQUAL® SPOONFUL*

*May substitute 6 packets EQUAL® sweetener.

• Peel and cut banana into large chunks. Place in plastic freezer bag; seal and freeze at least 5 to 6 hours or overnight.

• Place all ingredients in blender or food processor. Blend until smooth.

Makes 4 servings

Fruity Smoothie

1 **large ripe DOLE® Banana, peeled**

1 **can (8 ounces) DOLE® Pineapple Chunks, undrained**

1 **cup DOLE® Frozen Peaches, partially thawed**

1 **carton (6 ounces) peach low-fat yogurt**

Prep Time: 5 minutes

SLICE banana into blender or food processor container. Add pineapple, peaches and yogurt. Cover; blend until smooth.

Makes 3 servings

Variations: Replace 1 cup sliced peaches and peach yogurt with:

Blueberry: 1 cup DOLE® Frozen Blueberries and blueberry yogurt

Raspberry: 1 cup DOLE® Frozen Raspberries and mixed berry yogurt

Strawberry: 1 cup DOLE® Frozen Strawberries and strawberry yogurt

Mixed Berries: 1 cup DOLE® Frozen Mixed Berries and mixed berry yogurt

Blueberry Fruity Smoothie

Appetizers & Starters

ORTEGA® 7-Layer Dip

1 **can (16 ounces) ORTEGA® Refried Beans**

1 **packet (1.25 ounces) ORTEGA® Taco Seasoning Mix**

1 **container (8 ounces) sour cream**

1 **container (8 ounces) prepared guacamole**

1 **cup (4 ounces) shredded Cheddar cheese**

1 **cup ORTEGA® Salsa, any variety**

1 **can (4 ounces) ORTEGA® Fire-Roasted Diced Green Chiles**

2 **large green onions, sliced**

Tortilla chips

Prep Time: 10 minutes
Start to Finish Time: 10 minutes

COMBINE beans and seasoning mix in small bowl. Spread bean mixture in 8-inch square baking dish.

TOP with sour cream, guacamole, cheese, salsa, chiles and green onions, spreading each layer evenly in baking dish. Serve with chips.

Makes 10 to 12 servings

Note: This dip can be prepared and refrigerated up to 2 hours before serving.

Disappearing Buffalo Chicken Dip

2 **cups diced or shredded cooked chicken**

⅓ **cup cayenne pepper sauce**

1 **cup HELLMANN'S® or BEST FOODS® Real or Light Mayonnaise**

1 **cup shredded Cheddar cheese (about 4 ounces)**

2 **tablespoons finely chopped green onion (optional)**

1 **teaspoon lemon juice**

¼ **cup crumbled blue cheese**

Prep Time: 15 minutes
Cook Time: 20 minutes

1. Preheat oven to 375°F.

2. Toss chicken with cayenne pepper sauce. Stir in remaining ingredients except blue cheese. Turn into 1½-quart shallow casserole, then sprinkle with blue cheese.

3. Bake, uncovered, 20 minutes or until bubbling. Serve, if desired, with celery and/or your favorite dippers.

Makes 3 cups dip

FRANK'S® Sweet Chili Cream Cheese Dip

1 **package (8 ounces) PHILADELPHIA® Cream Cheese**

1 **cup FRANK'S® RedHot Sweet Chili® Sauce**

Prep Time: 5 minutes

PLACE cream cheese on serving dish.

POUR **FRANK'S RedHot** Sweet Chili Sauce evenly over cream cheese.

SERVE with crackers, chips or vegetables.

Makes 10 servings, 2 tablespoons each

TIP
You'll love this zesty dip—it's one of our most popular recipes!

Ultimate Party Meatballs

1 **can (16 ounces) OCEAN SPRAY® Jellied Cranberry Sauce**

1 **bottle (12 ounces) HEINZ® Chili Sauce**

2 **bags (1 pound each) frozen cocktail-size meatballs (about 64 meatballs)**

1. Combine Cranberry Sauce and Chili Sauce in a large saucepan. Cook over medium heat, whisking occasionally, until the cranberry sauce is melted and smooth.

2. Add meatballs; stir gently to coat. Cook over medium-low heat, stirring occasionally, 12 to 15 minutes or until meatballs are heated through. Place in chafing dish or slow cooker to keep warm.

Makes 30 servings

TIP

To spice it up even more, add a teaspoon of cumin and ¼ teaspoon ground red pepper to the sauce while it is cooking.

Slow Cooker Cheese Dip

1 pound ground beef

1 pound bulk Italian
    sausage

1 package (16 ounces)
    pasteurized process
    cheese product, cubed

1 can (11 ounces) sliced
    jalapeño peppers,
    drained

1 onion, chopped

8 ounces Cheddar cheese,
    cubed

1 package (8 ounces) cream
    cheese, cubed

1 container (8 ounces)
    cottage cheese

1 container (8 ounces) sour
    cream

1 can (about 14 ounces)
    diced tomatoes

3 cloves garlic, minced

    Salt and black pepper

    Tortilla chips

Cook Time: 1½ to 2 hours (HIGH)

1. Brown beef and sausage in large skillet 6 to 8 minutes over medium-high heat, stirring to break up meat. Remove to **CROCK-POT**® slow cooker using slotted spoon.

2. Add cheese product, jalapeño peppers, onion, Cheddar cheese, cream cheese, cottage cheese, sour cream, tomatoes and garlic to **CROCK-POT**® slow cooker; stir to blend. Cover; cook on HIGH 1½ to 2 hours. Season with salt and black pepper. Serve with chips.

Makes 16 to 18 servings

TIP

To reduce the fat in this recipe, use reduced-fat Cheddar cheese and Neufchâtel cheese instead of regular cream cheese.

BERTOLLI® Bruschetta

2 **loaves Italian or French bread, diagonally cut into ¾-inch slices**

2 **large cloves garlic**

⅓ **cup BERTOLLI® Extra Virgin Olive Oil**

1 **jar BERTOLLI® Tomato & Basil Sauce**

Bruschetta Toppings

Prep Time: 10 minutes
Cook Time: 5 minutes

Broil bread slices until golden in preheated oven; rub with garlic, then brush with BERTOLLI® Extra Virgin Olive Oil. Evenly spoon unheated BERTOLLI® Tomato & Basil Sauce over bread, then top with your favorite Bruschetta Toppings and enjoy!

Makes 24 servings

Bruschetta Toppings: Here are a few suggestions for Bruschetta Toppings or create your own!

• Sliced fresh mozzarella with chopped fresh basil.
• Sautéed sliced portobello mushrooms and fresh basil.
• Sliced fresh mozzarella with prosciutto and fresh basil.
• Sliced cooked chicken, feta cheese, olives and fresh thyme.
• Sliced fresh mozzarella with sliced or chopped roasted red peppers or sun-dried tomatoes and chopped fresh basil.

Chicken Kabobs with Thai Dipping Sauce

1 **pound boneless, skinless chicken breasts, cut into 1-inch cubes**

1 **small cucumber, halved, seeded and cut into thick slices**

1 **cup cherry tomatoes**

2 **green onions, cut into 1-inch pieces**

⅔ **cup teriyaki baste and glaze sauce**

⅓ **cup FRANK'S® RedHot® Original Cayenne Pepper Sauce**

⅓ **cup peanut butter**

3 **tablespoons frozen orange juice concentrate, undiluted**

2 **cloves garlic, minced**

Prep Time: 15 minutes
Cook Time: 10 minutes

THREAD chicken, cucumber, tomatoes and onions alternately onto metal skewers; set aside.

COMBINE teriyaki baste and glaze sauce, **FRANK'S RedHot** Original Cayenne Pepper Sauce, peanut butter, orange juice concentrate and garlic; mix well. Reserve ⅔ cup sauce for dipping.

BRUSH skewers with some of remaining sauce. Grill over medium-high heat 10 minutes or until chicken is no longer pink in center, turning and basting often with remaining sauce. Serve skewers with reserved Thai Dipping Sauce.

Makes 6 appetizer servings

Buffalo Chicken Wings

2½ **pounds chicken wing pieces**

¾ **cup any flavor FRANK'S® RedHot® Buffalo Wings Sauce**

Prep Time: 10 minutes
Cook Time: 20 minutes

BAKE wings in foil-lined pan at 500°F on lowest oven rack 20 to 25 minutes until crispy, turning once.

TOSS wings in **FRANK'S RedHot** Buffalo Wings Sauce to coat.

Makes 6 to 8 servings

Alternate Cooking Directions: Deep-fry at 375°F for 10 minutes or broil 6 inches from heat 15 to 20 minutes, turning once. Grill over medium heat 20 to 25 minutes, turning often.

TIP
You may substitute ½ cup **Frank's RedHot** Sauce mixed with ⅓ cup melted butter for the Wings Sauce.

Sauced Little Smokies

1 bottle (14 ounces) barbecue sauce

¾ cup grape jelly

½ cup packed brown sugar

½ cup reduced-sodium ketchup

1 tablespoon prepared mustard

1 teaspoon Worcestershire sauce

3 packages (14 to 16 ounces *each*) miniature turkey hot dogs

Cook Time:
3 to 4 hours (LOW)
1 to 2 hours (HIGH)

Stir barbecue sauce, jelly, brown sugar, ketchup, mustard and Worcestershire sauce into **CROCK-POT**® slow cooker until combined. Add hot dogs; stir to coat. Cover; cook on LOW 3 to 4 hours or on HIGH 1 to 2 hours.

Makes 24 servings

JOHNSONVILLE® Amazing Muffin Cups

3 **cups frozen hash browns, thawed**

3 **tablespoons melted butter**

⅛ **teaspoon salt**

⅛ **teaspoon black pepper**

12 **JOHNSONVILLE® Original Breakfast Sausage Links**

6 **eggs**

2 **cups (8 ounces) shredded Mexican cheese blend**

¼ **cup chopped red bell pepper**

Chopped fresh chives or green onions (optional)

Prep Time: 20 minutes
Bake Time: 25 to 30 minutes

1. Preheat oven to 400°F. Grease 12 standard (2½-inch) muffin pan cups or coat with nonstick cooking spray.

2. Combine hash browns, butter, salt and black pepper in large bowl. Press mixture evenly onto bottoms and up sides of prepared muffin cups. Bake 12 minutes or until lightly browned. Remove from oven.

3. Meanwhile, cook sausage according to package directions. When cool enough to handle, cut into ½-inch pieces; divide among muffin cups.

4. Whisk eggs in large bowl. Stir in cheese and bell pepper; mix well. Spoon evenly into muffin cups. Sprinkle with chives, if desired. Bake 13 to 15 minutes or until set.

Makes 12 servings

Party Meatballs

1 package (about 1 pound)
  frozen cocktail-size
  turkey or beef meatballs

½ cup maple syrup

1 jar (12 ounces) chili sauce

1 jar (12 ounces) grape jelly

Cook Time:
3 to 4 hours (LOW)
2 to 3 hours (HIGH)

Place meatballs, syrup, chili sauce and jelly in **CROCK-POT**® slow cooker; stir to blend. Cover; cook on LOW 3 to 4 hours or on HIGH 2 to 3 hours.

Makes 10 to 12 servings

Holiday Brie en Croute

1 **egg**

1 **tablespoon water**

½ **of a 17.3-ounce package PEPPERIDGE FARM® Puff Pastry Sheets (1 sheet), thawed**

½ **cup apricot preserves *or* seedless raspberry jam**

⅓ **cup dried cranberries**

¼ **cup toasted sliced almonds**

1 **(13- to 16-ounce) Brie cheese round**

1 **package (13 ounces) PEPPERIDGE FARM® Entertaining Quartet Distinctive Crackers**

Thaw Time: 40 minutes
Prep Time: 15 minutes
Bake Time: 20 minutes
Stand Time: 45 minutes

1. Heat the oven to 400°F. Beat the egg and water in a small bowl with a fork.

2. Unfold the pastry sheet on a lightly floured surface. Roll the pastry sheet into a 14-inch square. Spread the preserves on the pastry to within 2 inches of the edge. Sprinkle with the cranberries and almonds. Place the cheese in the center of the pastry. Fold the pastry up over the cheese to cover. Trim the excess pastry and press to seal. Brush the seam with the egg mixture. Place seam-side down onto a baking sheet. Decorate with the pastry scraps, if desired. Brush with the egg mixture.

3. Bake for 20 minutes or until the pastry is golden brown. Let stand for 45 minutes. Serve with the crackers.

Makes 12 servings

Soups & Chilies

Classic Chili

1½ **pounds ground beef**

1½ **cups chopped onion**

 1 **cup chopped green bell pepper**

 2 **cloves garlic, minced**

 3 **cans (about 15 ounces *each*) dark red kidney beans, rinsed and drained**

 2 **cans (about 15 ounces *each*) tomato sauce**

 1 **can (about 14 ounces) diced tomatoes**

 2 **to 3 teaspoons chili powder**

 1 **to 2 teaspoons ground mustard**

 ¾ **teaspoon dried basil**

 ½ **teaspoon black pepper**

 1 **to 2 dried red chiles (optional)**

Prep Time: 15 minutes
Cook Time:
8 to 10 hours (LOW)
4 to 5 hours (HIGH)

1. Brown beef, onion, bell pepper and garlic in large skillet over medium-high heat, stirring to break up meat. Remove beef mixture to **CROCK-POT**® slow cooker using slotted spoon.

2. Add beans, tomato sauce, tomatoes, chili powder, mustard, basil, black pepper and chiles, if desired, to **CROCK-POT**® slow cooker; mix well. Cover; cook on LOW 8 to 10 hours or on HIGH 4 to 5 hours. If used, remove chiles before serving.

Makes 6 servings

Tuscan White Bean Soup

- **2 tablespoons olive oil**
- **½ pound Italian-style chicken sausage *or* Italian-style turkey sausage, casing removed**
- **1 extra large onion, diced (about 1½ cups)**
- **½ cup dry white wine**
- **1 carton (32 ounces) SWANSON® Tuscan Chicken Flavor Infused Broth**
- **20 ounces kale (about 1 bunch), cut into thin strips (about 6 cups)**
- **1 can (about 15 ounces) canned white cannellini beans, rinsed and drained**
- **2 tablespoons chopped fresh parsley**
- **2 tablespoons grated Parmesan cheese (optional)**

Prep Time: 15 minutes
Cook Time: 30 minutes

1. Heat the oil in a 6-quart saucepot over medium-high heat. Add the sausage and cook until well browned, stirring often to separate the meat. Pour off any fat.

2. Add the onion to the saucepot and cook for 3 minutes, stirring occasionally. Add the wine to the saucepot and heat to a boil, stirring to scrape up the browned bits from the bottom of the saucepot. Cook for 2 minutes.

3. Stir in the broth and heat to a boil. Reduce the heat to medium-low. Stir in the kale and beans. Cover and cook for 10 minutes or until the kale is tender, stirring occasionally. Sprinkle with the parsley and cheese, if desired.

Makes 6 (about 1 cup) servings

Chili & Rice

- ¾ **pound ground beef (85% lean)**
- 1 **medium onion, chopped (about ½ cup)**
- 1 **tablespoon chili powder**
- 1 **can (10¾ ounces) CAMPBELL'S® Healthy Request® Condensed Tomato Soup**
- ¼ **cup water**
- 1 **teaspoon vinegar**
- 1 **can (about 15 ounces) kidney beans, rinsed and drained**
- 4 **cups hot cooked regular long-grain white rice, cooked without salt**

Prep Time: 10 minutes
Cook Time: 25 minutes

1. Cook the beef, onion and chili powder in a 10-inch skillet over medium-high heat until the beef is well browned, stirring often. Pour off any fat.

2. Stir the soup, water, vinegar and beans in the skillet and heat to a boil. Reduce the heat to low. Cook for 10 minutes or until the mixture is hot and bubbling. Serve the beef mixture over the rice.

Makes 4 servings

KITCHEN TIP

This dish is delicious served topped with shredded reduced-fat Cheddar cheese.

Easy Beef Stew

1½ **to 2 pounds cubed beef stew meat**

4 **medium potatoes, cubed**

4 **carrots, cut into 1½-inch pieces *or* 4 cups baby carrots**

1 **medium onion, cut into 8 pieces**

2 **cans (8 ounces *each*) tomato sauce**

1 **teaspoon salt**

½ **teaspoon black pepper**

Prep Time: 15 minutes
Cook Time:
8 to 10 hours (LOW)

Combine beef, potatoes, carrots, onion, tomato sauce, salt and pepper in **CROCK-POT**® slow cooker. Cover; cook on LOW 8 to 10 hours or until vegetables are tender.

Makes 6 to 8 servings

Sensational Chicken Noodle Soup

4 cups SWANSON® Chicken Broth (Regular, Natural Goodness® *or* Certified Organic)

Generous dash ground black pepper

1 medium carrot, sliced (about ½ cup)

1 stalk celery, sliced (about ½ cup)

½ cup *uncooked* extra-wide egg noodles

1 cup shredded cooked chicken *or* turkey

Prep Time: 5 minutes
Cook Time: 25 minutes

1. Heat the broth, black pepper, carrot and celery in a 2-quart saucepan over medium-high heat to a boil.

2. Stir the noodles and chicken into the saucepan. Reduce the heat to medium. Cook for 10 minutes or until the noodles are tender.

Makes 4 servings

Asian Soup: Add **2** green onions cut into ½-inch pieces, **1 clove** garlic, minced, **1 teaspoon** ground ginger and **2 teaspoons** soy sauce. Substitute **uncooked** curly Asian noodles for egg noodles.

Mexican Soup: Add ½ **cup** PACE® Chunky Salsa, **1 clove** garlic, minced, **1 cup** rinsed and drained black beans and ½ **teaspoon** chili powder. Substitute **2** corn tortillas (4- or 6-inch) cut into thin strips for the noodles, adding them just before serving.

Italian Tortellini Soup: Add **1 can** (about 14.5 ounces) diced tomatoes, drained, **1 clove** garlic, minced, **1 teaspoon** dried Italian seasoning, crushed, and **1 cup** spinach leaves. Substitute ½ **cup** frozen cheese tortellini for egg noodles. Serve with grated Parmesan cheese.

Quick and Zesty Vegetable Soup

1 lb. lean ground beef

½ cup chopped onion

Salt and pepper

2 cans (14.5 oz. each)
DEL MONTE® Italian
Recipe Stewed Tomatoes

2 cans (14 oz. each) beef
broth

1 can (14.5 oz.)
DEL MONTE® Mixed
Vegetables

½ cup uncooked medium
egg noodles

½ tsp. dried oregano

Prep Time: 5 minutes
Cook Time: 15 minutes

1. Brown meat with onion in large saucepan. Cook until onion is tender; drain. Season to taste with salt and pepper.

2. Stir in remaining ingredients. Bring to boil; reduce heat.

3. Cover and simmer 15 minutes or until noodles are tender.

Makes 8 servings

Barley and Lentil Soup

8 cups SWANSON® Beef Broth (Regular, 50% Less Sodium *or* Certified Organic)

2 cloves garlic, minced

1 teaspoon dried oregano leaves, crushed

4 large carrots, sliced (about 3 cups)

1 large onion, chopped (about 1 cup)

½ cup *uncooked* dried lentils

½ cup *uncooked* pearl barley

Prep Time: 10 minutes
Cook Time: 8 hours

1. Stir the broth, garlic, oregano, carrots, onion, lentils and barley in a 3½- to 6-quart slow cooker.

2. Cover and cook on LOW for 8 to 9 hours* or until the lentils and barley are tender.

*Or on HIGH for 4 to 5 hours.

Makes 8 servings

Creamy Chicken Tortilla Soup

1 cup PACE® Picante Sauce

2 cans (10¾ ounces *each*) CAMPBELL'S® Condensed Cream of Chicken Soup

1 pound skinless, boneless chicken breasts, cut into ½-inch pieces

2 cups frozen whole kernel corn

1 can (about 15 ounces) black beans, rinsed and drained

1 soup can water

1 teaspoon ground cumin

4 corn tortillas (6-inch), cut into strips

1 cup shredded Cheddar cheese (about 4 ounces)

⅓ cup chopped fresh cilantro leaves

Prep Time: 15 minutes
Cook Time: 4 hours 15 minutes

1. Stir the picante sauce, soup, chicken, corn, beans, water and cumin in a 4-quart slow cooker.

2. Cover and cook on LOW for 4 to 5 hours* or until the chicken is cooked through.

3. Stir the tortillas, cheese and cilantro in the cooker. Cover and cook for 15 minutes. Serve with additional cheese, if desired.

*Or on HIGH for 2 to 2½ hours.

Makes 6 servings

Santa Fe Turkey Chili

1   **tablespoon vegetable oil**

1   **cup onion, chopped**

2   **cloves garlic, chopped**

1   **tablespoon chili powder**

1   **(16-ounce) can whole tomatoes, undrained and cut-up**

1   **(15-ounce) can herbed tomato sauce**

1   **(16-ounce) can red kidney beans, drained**

1   **cup frozen whole kernel corn**

2   **cups JENNIE-O TURKEY STORE® Turkey, cooked and cubed**

¼   **teaspoon or to taste cayenne pepper (optional)**

Yogurt, shredded cheese, sliced green onion and warm corn tortillas (optional)

Prep Time: 30 minutes
Cook Time: 30 minutes

In Dutch oven or large saucepan over medium-high heat, heat oil until hot. Cook onion and garlic until tender. Stir in chili powder. Add tomatoes with juice, tomato sauce, beans and corn. Reduce heat to low; cover and simmer 10 minutes, stirring occasionally. Uncover, add turkey and cayenne pepper, if desired; simmer 5 minutes longer. Serve with yogurt, cheese, green onion and tortillas, if desired.

Makes 6 servings

French Onion Soup

¼ cup (½ stick) butter

3 pounds yellow onions, sliced

1 tablespoon sugar

2 to 3 tablespoons dry white wine or water (optional)

8 cups beef broth

8 to 16 slices French bread (optional)

½ cup (2 ounces) shredded Gruyère or Swiss cheese

Prep Time: 20 minutes
Cook Time:
8 hours (LOW)
6 hours (HIGH)

1. Melt butter in large skillet over medium-low heat. Add onions; cover and cook just until onions are tender and transparent, but not browned, about 10 minutes.

2. Remove cover. Sprinkle sugar over onions. Cook and stir 8 to 10 minutes or until onions are caramelized. Add onions and any browned bits to **CROCK-POT**® slow cooker. If desired, add wine to skillet. Bring to a boil, scraping up any browned bits. Add to **CROCK-POT**® slow cooker. Stir in broth. Cover; cook on LOW 8 hours or on HIGH 6 hours.

3. Preheat broiler. To serve, ladle soup into individual soup bowls. If desired, top each with 1 or 2 bread slices and about 1 tablespoon cheese. Place under broiler until cheese is melted and bubbly.

Makes 8 servings

Variation: Substitute 1 cup dry white wine for 1 cup of beef broth.

Italian Wedding Soup

TINY MEATBALLS

- **1 package (19 ounces) JOHNSONVILLE® Mild Italian Sausage Links, casings removed***
- **1 cup bread crumbs (plain or seasoned)**
- **1 egg, lightly beaten**
- **1 tablespoon minced fresh Italian parsley**
- **2 teaspoons crushed fennel seeds**
- **⅛ teaspoon ground red pepper (optional)**

SOUP

- **8 ounces uncooked orzo pasta**
- **2 tablespoons extra-virgin olive oil**
- **1 medium onion, finely diced**
- **1 teaspoon chopped fresh thyme leaves or ½ teaspoon dried thyme**
- **1 teaspoon dried sage**
- **1 medium carrot, finely chopped**
- **1 stalk celery, finely chopped**
- **2 cloves garlic, finely minced**
- **8 cups chicken broth or stock**
- **1 bay leaf**
- **1 cup roughly chopped fresh spinach**
- **⅓ cup shredded Parmesan cheese**

*Cut sausage link end to end, about three-quarters of the way through; open and flip sausage link over, then grasp casing and pull off.

1. Combine all meatball ingredients in large bowl; mix well. Roll mixture into small marble-size meatballs. If forming meatballs is difficult, cover mixture and refrigerate until firm.

2. Cook pasta according to package directions until al dente. Drain; set aside.

3. Heat oil in large soup pot over medium heat. Add onion, thyme and sage; cook and stir 5 to 7 minutes or until onion starts to turn golden. Add carrot, celery and garlic; cook and stir 5 minutes. Transfer vegetables to plate; set aside.

4. Add meatballs to soup pot; cook 2 to 3 minutes before stirring (to keep meatballs from breaking). Gently turn meatballs until browned on all sides.

5. Add reserved vegetables, broth and bay leaf. Simmer gently (do not boil), until vegetables are tender and meatballs are cooked through. Stir in cooked pasta and spinach. Sprinkle with cheese before serving.

Makes 6 to 8 servings

TIP
Adding chopped spinach right before serving the soup will help the spinach maintain its rich green color.

Prep Time: 25 minutes
Cook Time: 40 minutes

Salads & Sides

Crunchy Mexican Side Salad

3 **cups romaine and iceberg lettuce blend**

½ **cup grape tomato halves**

½ **cup peeled and diced jicama**

¼ **cup B&G® Sliced Ripe Olives**

¼ **cup ORTEGA® Sliced Jalapeños, quartered**

2 **tablespoons ORTEGA® Taco Sauce, any variety**

1 **tablespoon vegetable oil**

⅛ **teaspoon salt**

Crushed ORTEGA® Taco Shells, any variety (optional)

Prep Time: 5 minutes
Start to Finish: 10 minutes

TOSS together lettuce, tomatoes, jicama, olives and jalapeños in large bowl.

COMBINE taco sauce, oil and salt in small bowl. Stir with fork until blended.

POUR dressing over salad; toss gently to coat. Top with taco shells, if desired.

Makes 4 servings (1 cup each)

Note: ORTEGA® Sliced Jalapeños are available in a 12-ounce jar. They are pickled, adding great flavor and crunch to this salad.

Loaded Potato Potluck Favorite

8 medium potatoes (about 2½ to 3 pounds *total*), peeled and cut into 1-inch chunks

1 cup NESTLÉ® CARNATION® Evaporated Milk

½ cup sour cream

1 teaspoon salt

½ teaspoon ground black pepper

2 cups (8-ounce package) shredded cheddar cheese, *divided*

6 slices bacon, cooked and crumbled, *divided*

Sliced green onions (optional)

Prep Time: 15 minutes
Cooking Time: 45 minutes

PLACE potatoes in large saucepan. Cover with water; bring to a boil. Cook over medium-high heat for 15 to 20 minutes or until tender; drain.

PREHEAT oven to 350°F. Grease 2½- to 3-quart casserole dish.

RETURN potatoes to saucepan; add evaporated milk, sour cream, salt and pepper. Beat with hand-held mixer until smooth. Stir in 1½ *cups* cheese and *half* of bacon. Spoon mixture into prepared casserole dish.

BAKE for 20 to 25 minutes or until heated through. Top with *remaining ½ cup* cheese, *remaining* bacon and green onions. Bake for an additional 3 minutes or until cheese is melted.

Makes 16 servings (½ cup *each*)

 TIP

This casserole can be assembled ahead of time and refrigerated. Cover with foil and bake at 350°F for 40 to 45 minutes or until heated. Uncover; top with cheese, bacon and green onions; bake for an additional 3 minutes or until cheese is melted.

Lemon Herb Broccoli Casserole

1 can (10¾ ounces)
  CAMPBELL'S®
  Condensed Cream of
  Chicken with Herbs Soup

½ cup milk

1 tablespoon lemon juice

4 cups frozen broccoli cuts,
  thawed

1 can (2.8 ounces) French
  fried onions (1⅓ cups)

Prep Time: 10 minutes
Cook Time: 30 minutes

1. Stir the soup, milk, lemon juice, broccoli and ⅔ **cup** onions in a 1½-quart casserole. Cover the casserole.

2. Bake at 350°F. for 25 minutes or until the broccoli is tender. Stir the broccoli mixture. Sprinkle with the remaining onions.

3. Bake, uncovered, for 5 minutes or until the onions are golden brown.

Makes 6 servings

KITCHEN TIP

To thaw the broccoli, microwave on HIGH for 3 minutes.

Honey-Glazed Carrots

1 **pound carrots, sliced**

3 **tablespoons COUNTRY CROCK® Honey Spread or COUNTRY CROCK® Spread, divided**

¼ **cup finely chopped onion**

2 **teaspoons sugar**

¼ **teaspoon salt**

Prep Time: 5 minutes
Cook Time: 15 minutes

1. Cover carrots with 1-inch water in 10-inch nonstick skillet. Bring to a boil over high heat. Reduce heat to low and simmer covered until crisp-tender, about 8 minutes; drain.

2. Return carrots to skillet. Add 2 tablespoons COUNTRY CROCK® Honey Spread and remaining ingredients and cook, stirring occasionally, until carrots are tender, about 5 minutes. To serve, top with remaining 1 tablespoon Spread.

Makes 4 servings

Sweet Potato & Pumpkin Casserole

CASSEROLE

- **4 pounds sweet potatoes, scrubbed and cut into 2- to 3-inch pieces**
- **1 can (15 ounces) LIBBY'S® 100% Pure Pumpkin**
- **¼ cup packed brown sugar**
- **3 tablespoons butter, softened**
- **1 teaspoon kosher salt**
- **1 teaspoon freshly ground black pepper**
- **2 large eggs**

TOPPING

- **⅓ cup packed brown sugar**
- **3 tablespoons all-purpose flour**
- **1 tablespoon butter, melted Pinch of salt**
- **½ cup chopped pecans**

Prep Time: 15 minutes
Cooking Time: 41 minutes
Cooling Time: 10 minutes

PREHEAT oven to 350°F.

FOR CASSEROLE

PLACE potatoes on microwave-safe plate. Microwave on HIGH (100%) power for 15 minutes or until potatoes are tender. Cool slightly; place in large bowl. Add pumpkin, sugar, butter, salt and pepper. With potato masher, smash until lumpy (cut any large pieces of skin into smaller pieces). Add eggs; smash until incorporated. Spoon into 13×9-inch or 3-quart baking dish.

FOR TOPPING

COMBINE sugar, flour, butter and salt in small bowl; stir until combined. Sprinkle evenly over casserole; top evenly with nuts.

BAKE for 25 minutes or until golden and heated through. Remove from oven.

PREHEAT broiler. Broil casserole for 1 minute or until bubbly and nuts are toasted. Cool for 5 minutes before serving.

Makes 18 servings (½ cup *each*)

Easy Tossed Niçoise with Garlic and Cheese Dressing

1½ **pounds steamed red potatoes, cut into small chunks**

1 **package (10 ounces) frozen Italian green beans, thawed and drained**

¾ **cup niçoise or pitted ripe olives, sliced**

½ **red onion, slivered**

½ **red bell pepper, slivered**

½ **green bell pepper, slivered**

¼ **cup coarsely chopped green onions, including tops**

1½ **cups Garlic and Cheese Dressing (recipe follows)**

1 **(6.4-ounce) STARKIST Flavor Fresh Pouch® Tuna (Albacore)**

½ **cup minced fresh parsley**

Whole romaine leaves, washed and dried

Freshly ground black pepper (optional)

Grated Parmesan cheese (optional)

Prep Time: 15 minutes

In large bowl, combine potatoes, beans, olives, red onion, bell peppers and green onions; toss with Garlic and Cheese Dressing. Refrigerate. Just before serving, add tuna and parsley. Line plates with lettuce; spoon salad onto leaves. Serve with black pepper and cheese, if desired.

Makes 6 to 8 servings

Garlic and Cheese Dressing

¼ **cup wine vinegar**

2 **tablespoons lemon juice**

1 **tablespoon Dijon-style mustard**

1 **to 2 cloves garlic, minced or pressed**

Salt and black pepper to taste

1 **cup olive oil**

½ **cup grated Parmesan cheese**

In small bowl, whisk together vinegar, lemon juice, mustard, garlic, salt and pepper. Slowly add olive oil, whisking until all oil is added and dressing is thickened. Stir in cheese.

Herbed Garlic Bread

¼ cup **COUNTRY CROCK® Calcium plus Vitamin D or COUNTRY CROCK® Spread**

1 teaspoon **dried herbs, crushed, or 1 tablespoon finely chopped fresh herbs**

½ teaspoon **garlic powder**

1 loaf **French or Italian bread (about 12 ounces), sliced lengthwise**

Prep Time: 10 minutes
Cook Time: 2 minutes

Combine all ingredients except bread in small bowl. Arrange bread on baking sheet; spread with herb mixture. Broil* until golden.

*Bake aluminum foil-wrapped bread at 425°F for 25 minutes.

Makes 6 servings

Loaded Baked Potato Casserole

1 bag (32 ounces)
   Southern-style hash-
   brown potatoes, thawed
   (about 7½ cups)

1 can (6 ounces) French
   fried onions (2⅔ cups)

1 cup frozen peas, thawed

1 cup shredded Cheddar
   cheese (4 ounces)

4 slices bacon, cooked and
   crumbled

2 cans (10¾ ounces
   each) CAMPBELL'S®
   Condensed Cream of
   Celery Soup (Regular *or*
   98% Fat Free)

1 cup milk

Prep Time: 15 minutes
Cook Time: 35 minutes

1. Stir the potatoes, **1⅓ cups** of the onions, peas, cheese and bacon in a 13×9-inch (3-quart) shallow baking dish. Stir the soup and milk in a medium bowl. Pour the soup mixture over the potato mixture. **Cover**.

2. Bake at 350°F. for 30 minutes or until hot. Stir.

3. Sprinkle with the remaining onions. Bake for 5 minutes more or until the onions are golden brown.

Makes 8 servings

KITCHEN TIP
To thaw the hash browns, cut off 1 corner on bag and microwave on HIGH for 5 minutes.

Asian Shrimp & Noodle Salad

⅓ cup plus 2 tablespoons
  vegetable oil, divided

¼ cup cider vinegar

2 tablespoons FRENCH'S®
  Worcestershire Sauce

2 tablespoons light soy
  sauce

2 tablespoons honey

1 teaspoon grated fresh
  ginger or ¼ teaspoon
  ground ginger

2 packages (3 ounces each)
  chicken-flavor ramen
  noodle soup

1 pound shrimp, cleaned
  and deveined with tails
  left on

2 cups vegetables such as
  broccoli, carrots and
  snow peas, cut into bite-
  size pieces

1⅓ cups FRENCH'S® French
  Fried Onions, divided

Prep Time: 15 minutes
Cook Time: 10 minutes

1. Combine ⅓ cup oil, vinegar, Worcestershire, soy sauce, honey and ginger until well blended; set aside. Prepare ramen noodles according to package directions for soup; drain and rinse noodles. Place in large serving bowl.

2. Stir-fry shrimp in 1 tablespoon oil in large skillet over medium-high heat, stirring constantly, until shrimp turn pink. Remove shrimp to bowl with noodles. Stir-fry vegetables in remaining oil in skillet over medium-high heat, stirring constantly, until vegetables are crisp-tender.

3. Add vegetable mixture, dressing and 1 cup French Fried Onions to bowl with noodles; toss to coat well. Serve immediately topped with remaining ⅓ cup onions.

Makes 6 servings

TIP
Purchase cut-up vegetables from the salad bar of your local supermarket to save prep time.

Ultra Creamy Mashed Potatoes

3½ cups **SWANSON® Chicken Broth (Regular, Natural Goodness® or Certified Organic)**

5 **large potatoes, cut into 1-inch pieces (about 7½ cups)**

½ **cup light cream**

2 **tablespoons butter**

Generous dash ground black pepper

1 **can (14½ ounces) CAMPBELL'S® Turkey Gravy**

Prep Time: 15 minutes
Cook Time: 20 minutes

1. Heat the broth and potatoes in a 3-quart saucepan over medium-high heat to a boil.

2. Reduce the heat to medium. Cover and cook for 10 minutes or until the potatoes are tender. Drain, reserving the broth.

3. Mash the potatoes with ¼ **cup** broth, cream, butter and black pepper. Add additional broth, if needed, until desired consistency. Serve with the gravy.

Makes 6 servings

Ultimate Mashed Potatoes: Stir ½ **cup** sour cream, **3** slices bacon, cooked and crumbled (reserve some for garnish), and ¼ **cup** chopped fresh chives into the hot mashed potatoes. Sprinkle with the reserved bacon.

Easy Fried Rice

¼ cup vegetable oil

4 cups cooked rice

2 cloves garlic, finely
  chopped

1 envelope LIPTON®
  RECIPE SECRETS® Onion
  Mushroom Soup Mix

½ cup water

1 tablespoon soy sauce

1 cup frozen peas and
  carrots, partially thawed

2 eggs, lightly beaten

Prep Time: 10 minutes
Cook Time: 10 minutes

1. In 12-inch nonstick skillet, heat olive oil over medium-high heat and cook rice, stirring constantly, 2 minutes or until rice is heated through. Stir in garlic.

2. Stir in soup mix blended with water and soy sauce and cook 1 minute. Stir in peas and carrots and cook 2 minutes or until heated through.

3. Make a well in center of rice and quickly stir in eggs until cooked.

Makes 4 servings

Moist & Savory Stuffing

2½ cups **SWANSON® Chicken Broth (Regular, Natural Goodness® *or* Certified Organic)**

Generous dash ground black pepper

2 **stalks celery, coarsely chopped (about 1 cup)**

1 **large onion, coarsely chopped (about 1 cup)**

1 **package (16 ounces) PEPPERIDGE FARM® Herb Seasoned Stuffing**

Prep Time: 10 minutes
Cook Time: 10 minutes
Bake Time: 30 minutes

1. Heat the broth, black pepper, celery and onion in a 3-quart saucepan over medium-high heat to a boil. Reduce the heat to low. Cover and cook for 5 minutes or until the vegetables are tender, stirring often. Remove the saucepan from the heat. Add the stuffing and mix lightly.

2. Spoon the stuffing mixture into a greased 3-quart shallow baking dish. Cover the baking dish.

3. Bake at 350°F. for 30 minutes or until the stuffing is hot.

Makes 10 servings

Cranberry & Pecan Stuffing: Stir ½ **cup each** dried cranberries **and** chopped pecans into the stuffing mixture.

Sausage & Mushroom Stuffing: Add **1 cup** sliced mushrooms to the vegetables during cooking. Stir ½ **pound** pork sausage, cooked and crumbled, into the stuffing mixture before baking.

KITCHEN TIP
For crunchier stuffing, bake the casserole uncovered.

Honey Apple BBQ Sauce

1 cup **HEINZ**® **Tomato
  Ketchup**

1 cup **applesauce**

2 tablespoons **honey**

¼ teaspoon **ground
  cinnamon**

Prep Time: 5 minutes
Cook Time: 10 minutes

1. In a small saucepan, combine Ketchup, applesauce, honey and cinnamon. Bring to a boil. Reduce heat and simmer, uncovered, 5 minutes, stirring occasionally.

2. Brush frequently on chicken, pork or turkey during last 10 minutes of grilling. Heat any remaining sauce to boiling and cook 2 minutes. Use as a dipping sauce.

Makes 12 servings

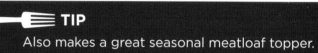

TIP

Also makes a great seasonal meatloaf topper.

Chicken Mandarin Salad

3 cups diced cooked chicken or turkey

1 can (15 oz.) DEL MONTE® Mandarin Oranges No Sugar Added, drained

¼ cup slivered almonds, toasted*

¼ cup light mayonnaise

¼ cup low-fat plain yogurt

1 Tbsp. honey

2 Tbsp. lemon or lime juice (optional)

1 tsp. grated lemon or lime peel

Lettuce (optional)

*To toast almonds, spread in single layer in heavy skillet. Cook over medium heat 1 to 2 minutes or until nuts are lightly browned, stirring frequently.

Prep Time: 15 minutes
Chill Time: 30 minutes

1. Combine chicken, oranges and almonds in medium salad bowl.

2. Thoroughly blend mayonnaise, yogurt, honey, juice, if desired, and lemon peel.

3. Toss gently with chicken mixture. Chill and serve on lettuce-lined plates, if desired.

Makes 5 servings

Cheddar Potato Casserole

3 cups prepared mashed
  potatoes

1 can (10¾ ounces)
  CAMPBELL'S® Condensed
  Cheddar Cheese Soup

⅓ cup sour cream *or* yogurt

  Generous dash ground
  black pepper

1 green onion, chopped
  (about 2 tablespoons)

Prep Time: 10 minutes
Bake Time: 30 minutes

1. Stir the potatoes, soup, sour cream, black pepper and onion in a medium bowl. Spoon the potato mixture into a 1½-quart baking dish.

2. Bake at 350°F. for 30 minutes or until the potato mixture is hot.

Makes 8 servings

🍴≣ KITCHEN TIP

To make **3 cups** mashed potatoes, place **2 pounds** potatoes, peeled and cut into 1-inch pieces, into a 3-quart saucepan. Add water to cover and heat over medium-high heat to a boil. Reduce the heat to low. Cover and cook for 10 minutes or until the potatoes are tender. Drain. Mash the potatoes with ¾ **cup** milk and **2 tablespoons** butter.

Broccoli Bake

1 can (10¾ ounces)
  CAMPBELL'S® Condensed
  Cream of Mushroom Soup
  (Regular *or* 98% Fat Free)

½ cup milk

1 teaspoon soy sauce

  Generous dash ground
  black pepper

2 packages (10 ounces *each*)
  frozen broccoli cuts *or*
  4 cups fresh broccoli
  florets, cooked and
  drained

1⅓ cups French fried onions

Prep Time: 10 minutes
Bake Time: 30 minutes

1. Stir the soup, milk, soy sauce, black pepper, broccoli and ⅔ **cup** onions in a 1½-quart casserole.

2. Bake at 350°F. for 25 minutes or until it's hot and bubbling. Stir the mixture.

3. Top with the remaining onions. Bake for 5 minutes or until the onions are golden.

Makes 6 servings

KITCHEN TIPS

The recipe may be doubled. Use a 2-quart shallow baking dish and increase the baking time to 30 minutes plus 5 minutes.

You can also use CAMPBELL'S® Condensed Cream of Broccoli Soup, for even more broccoli flavor, in place of the Cream of Mushroom Soup.

Sweet Potato Casserole

SWEET POTATOES

Softened butter, for the casserole

3 cups canned mashed sweet potatoes (one 29-ounce can and one 16-ounce can, drained), or 2 pounds fresh sweet potatoes, baked or peeled and boiled, then mashed

1 cup granulated sugar

1 stick (¼ pound) butter, melted

2 large eggs

½ cup evaporated milk

1 teaspoon ground cinnamon

1 teaspoon vanilla extract

TOPPING

1½ cups packed brown sugar

⅔ cup self-rising flour

1½ sticks (12 tablespoons) cold butter, cut into bits

1½ cups coarsely chopped pecans

1. Preheat oven to 350°F. Lightly butter the casserole.

2. Make the sweet potatoes: In a large bowl, combine the mashed sweet potatoes, granulated sugar, melted butter, eggs, evaporated milk, cinnamon, and vanilla. Spoon into the casserole.

3. Make the topping: In a large bowl, combine the brown sugar and flour. With a pastry blender, cut in the butter and pecans. Scatter the topping over the sweet potatoes.

4. Bake 1 hour or until the topping is crisp and the potatoes are piping hot.

Makes 10 to 12 servings

Green Bean Casserole

1 can (10¾ ounces)
 CAMPBELL'S®
 Condensed Cream
 of Mushroom Soup
 (Regular *or* 98% Fat
 Free)

½ cup milk

1 teaspoon soy sauce

 Dash ground black
 pepper

2 packages (10 ounces
 each) frozen cut green
 beans, cooked and
 drained

1 can (2.8 ounces) French
 fried onions (1⅓ cups)

Prep Time: 10 minutes
Bake Time: 30 minutes

1. Stir the soup, milk, soy sauce, black pepper, green beans and ⅔ **cup** onions in a 1½-quart casserole.

2. Bake at 350°F. for 25 minutes or until hot. Stir the green bean mixture.

3. Sprinkle the remaining onions over the green bean mixture. Bake for 5 minutes more or until onions are golden brown.

Makes 5 servings

KITCHEN TIP

You can also make this classic side dish with fresh or canned green beans. You will need either **1½ pounds** fresh green beans, cut into 1-inch pieces, cooked and drained, or **2 cans** (about 16 ounces **each**) cut green beans, drained, for the frozen green beans.

Tangy Apple Slaw

4 cups shredded green cabbage

1 cup shredded carrots

1 cup chopped unpeeled apple (1 medium)

½ cup thinly sliced red or green bell pepper strips

⅔ cup light mayonnaise or salad dressing

⅓ cup reduced-fat sour cream

3 tablespoons EQUAL® SPOONFUL*

1½ tablespoons Dijon mustard

1 tablespoon lemon juice

⅛ teaspoon pepper

*May substitute 4½ packets EQUAL® sweetener.

• Combine cabbage, carrots, apple and bell pepper in medium bowl.

• Mix mayonnaise, sour cream, EQUAL®, mustard, lemon juice and pepper in small bowl; stir until well blended.

• Spoon Equal® mixture over cabbage mixture; gently toss to combine.

• Refrigerate, covered, 1 to 2 hours to allow flavors to blend.

Makes 6 servings

Twice Baked Potatoes

3 hot baked potatoes, split lengthwise

½ cup sour cream

2 tablespoons butter or margarine

1⅓ cups FRENCH'S® French Fried Onions, divided

1 cup (4 ounces) shredded Cheddar cheese, divided

Dash paprika (optional)

Prep Time: 10 minutes
Cook Time: 22 minutes

1. Preheat oven to 400°F. Scoop out inside of potatoes into medium bowl, leaving thin shells. Mash potatoes with sour cream and butter until smooth. Stir in ⅔ *cup* French Fried Onions and ½ *cup* cheese. Spoon mixture into shells.

2. Bake 20 minutes or until heated through. Top with remaining cheese, onions and paprika, if desired. Bake 2 minutes or until cheese melts.

Makes 6 servings

Variation: For added Cheddar flavor, substitute **FRENCH'S® Cheddar French Fried Onions** for the original flavor.

TIP
To bake potatoes quickly, microwave on HIGH 10 to 12 minutes until tender.

Ambrosia

1 can (20 ounces) DOLE®
  Pineapple Chunks,
  drained or 2 cups DOLE®
  Frozen Tropical Gold
  Pineapple Chunks,
  partially thawed

1 can (11 or 15 ounces)
  DOLE® Mandarin
  Oranges, drained

1 DOLE® Banana, sliced

1½ cups seedless grapes

½ cup miniature
  marshmallows

1 cup vanilla low fat yogurt

¼ cup flaked coconut,
  toasted

Prep Time: 15 minutes

• Combine pineapple chunks, mandarin oranges, banana, grapes and marshmallows in medium bowl.

• Stir yogurt into fruit mixture. Sprinkle with coconut.

Makes 4 to 6 servings

Main Dishes

Yankee Pot Roast

1 **boneless beef chuck pot roast (arm, shoulder or blade), about 2½ pounds**

⅓ **cup all-purpose flour**

¾ **teaspoon salt**

¾ **teaspoon pepper**

1 **tablespoon vegetable oil**

1 **can (14 to 14½ ounces) beef broth**

½ **cup dry red wine**

1½ **teaspoons dried thyme leaves, crushed**

2 **packages (16 ounces** *each*) **frozen stew vegetable mixture (such as potatoes, carrots, celery and onion)**

Prep and Cook Time:
3 to 3½ hours

1. Combine flour, salt and pepper. Lightly coat beef in 2 tablespoons of the flour mixture. Heat oil in large stockpot over medium heat until hot. Place beef pot roast in stockpot; brown evenly. Pour off drippings.

2. Combine beef broth, red wine, thyme and remaining flour mixture; add to stockpot and bring to a boil. Reduce heat; cover tightly and simmer 2 hours. Add vegetables to stockpot; continue simmering 30 to 45 minutes or until pot roast and vegetables are fork-tender.

3. Remove pot roast and vegetables; keep warm. Skim fat from cooking liquid, if necessary.

4. Cut pot roast into bite-size pieces. Serve with vegetables and gravy.

Makes 6 servings

Courtesy: The Beef Checkoff

Soup-erb Chicken Casserole

1 **can (10¾ ounces) CAMPBELL'S® Condensed Cream of Broccoli Soup (Regular** *or* **98% Fat Free)**

1 **cup milk**

½ **cup shredded mozzarella cheese**

¼ **teaspoon garlic powder**

⅛ **teaspoon ground black pepper**

2 **cups cubed cooked chicken** *or* **turkey**

1 **package (10 ounces) frozen peas and carrots, cooked and drained**

1 **cup elbow macaroni, cooked and drained**

½ **cup PEPPERIDGE FARM® Herb Seasoned Stuffing, crushed**

2 **tablespoons grated Parmesan cheese**

2 **tablespoons butter**

Prep Time: 15 minutes
Cook Time: 25 minutes

1. Heat the oven to 400°F.

2. Stir the soup, milk, mozzarella cheese, garlic powder and black pepper in 11×8-inch (2-quart) shallow baking dish. Stir in the chicken, peas and carrots and macaroni.

3. Bake for 20 minutes. **Stir.**

4. Mix the stuffing, Parmesan cheese and butter in a small bowl. Sprinkle over the chicken mixture. Bake for 5 minutes more or until hot.

Makes 8 servings

KITCHEN TIP

An easy way to crush the stuffing is to place it in a resealable bag and seal. Use a rolling pin and roll back and forth over the bag until the stuffing is crushed.

Lean Mean Cheeseburger

1 **pound ground beef (95% lean)**

2 **tablespoons quick-cooking oats**

½ **teaspoon steak seasoning blend**

4 **seeded *or* whole wheat hamburger buns, split**

4 **slices lowfat cheese, such as Cheddar *or* American**

TOPPINGS

Lettuce leaves, tomato slices (optional)

Prep and Cook Time: 20 minutes

1. Place oats in foodsafe plastic bag. Seal bag securely, squeezing out excess air. Roll over bag with rolling pin to crush oats to a fine consistency.

2. Combine ground beef, oats and steak seasoning blend in large bowl, mixing lightly but thoroughly. Lightly shape into four ½-inch patties.

3. Place patties on grid over medium, ash-covered coals. Grill, covered, 11 to 13 minutes (over medium heat on preheated gas grill, covered, 7 to 8 minutes) until instant-read thermometer inserted horizontally into center registers 160°F, turning occasionally.

4. Line bottom of each bun with lettuce and tomato, if desired; top with burger and cheese slice. Close sandwiches.

Makes 4 servings

Courtesy: The Beef Checkoff

COOK'S TIP

Cooking times are for fresh or thoroughly thawed ground beef. Color is not a reliable indicator of ground beef doneness.

Chicken Sorrento

1 tablespoon vegetable oil

1 pound skinless, boneless chicken breast halves

1 jar (24 ounces) PREGO® Veggie Smart® Chunky & Savory Italian Sauce

2 tablespoons balsamic vinegar

2 tablespoons chopped fresh basil leaves

3 cups penne pasta, cooked and drained (about 4½ cups)

¼ cup grated Parmesan cheese

Prep Time: 30 minutes
Cook Time: 20 minutes

1. Heat the oil in a 10-inch skillet over medium-high heat. Add the chicken and cook for 10 minutes or until well browned on both sides. Remove the chicken from the skillet.

2. Stir the Italian sauce and vinegar in the skillet and cook for 2 minutes, stirring often. Stir in the basil. Return the chicken to the skillet. Reduce the heat to low. Cover and cook for 5 minutes or until the chicken is cooked through.

3. Slice the chicken. Serve the chicken and sauce over the penne. Sprinkle with the cheese.

Makes 4 servings

Turkey Breast and Sweet Potatoes

1 tablespoon all-purpose flour

1 (6-pound) BUTTERBALL® Fresh or Frozen Whole Turkey Breast, thawed if frozen

3 large sweet potatoes, peeled and cut into 1-inch slices

2 medium Granny Smith apples, peeled and chopped

1 medium onion, sliced and separated into rings

½ cup frozen apple juice concentrate, thawed

1 teaspoon soy sauce

1 teaspoon dried thyme

½ teaspoon coarsely ground black pepper

¼ cup water

2 tablespoons cornstarch

Prep Time: 30 minutes
Cook Time: 2 hours

1. Preheat oven to 350°F. Add flour to large oven-cooking bag; close and shake to coat inside of bag. Place bag in 15×10-inch baking pan.

2. Remove gravy packet from turkey breast. Refrigerate for another use or discard. Pat turkey dry with paper towels; place in oven-cooking bag. Add potatoes, apples and onion.

3. Combine juice concentrate, soy sauce, thyme and pepper in small bowl; mix well. Pour over ingredients in bag. Close bag with tie; cut 6 (½-inch-long) slits in top of bag to vent.

4. Roast turkey 1½ to 1¾ hours or until meat thermometer reaches 170°F when inserted into thickest part of breast. Remove from oven. Let stand 5 minutes.

5. Cut bag open carefully. Transfer turkey to cutting board; loosely tent with foil. Place sweet potatoes on serving platter; cover to keep warm. Pour juices from bag into 1-quart microwavable cup or bowl (there should be about 2 cups); discard bag. Stir water and cornstarch in small bowl until smooth; stir into juices. Microwave on HIGH 2½ minutes or until thickened, stirring in 1-minute intervals. Serve with turkey and sweet potatoes.

Makes 8 servings

Parmesan Crusted Chicken

½ **cup HELLMANN'S® or BEST FOODS® Light Mayonnaise**

¼ **cup grated Parmesan cheese**

4 **boneless, skinless chicken breast halves (about 1¼ pounds)**

4 **teaspoons Italian seasoned dry bread crumbs**

Prep Time: 10 minutes
Cook Time: 20 minutes

1. Preheat oven to 425°F.

2. Combine HELLMANN'S® or BEST FOODS® Light Mayonnaise with cheese in medium bowl. Arrange chicken on baking sheet. Evenly top with mayonnaise mixture, then sprinkle with bread crumbs.

3. Bake 20 minutes or until chicken is thoroughly cooked.

Makes 4 servings

Variation: Also terrific with HELLMANN'S® or BEST FOODS® Canola Cholesterol Free Mayonnaise.

TIPS

Try making this dish with thin-cut boneless skinless chicken breasts! Prepare as above, decreasing bake time to 10 minutes or until chicken is thoroughly cooked.

Omit Parmesan cheese and have "Magically Moist Chicken" on the table in less than 30 minutes.

MASTERBUILT® Smokin' Fried Turkey

50/50 mixture apple juice and water

1 (10- to 12-pound) BUTTERBALL® fresh or frozen whole turkey, thawed if frozen

1 (16-ounce) jar plus (8 ounces) BUTTERBALL® Buttery Creole Injection Marinade or our favorite marinade

1 (3.7-ounce) package BUTTERBALL® Cajun Seasoning or your favorite Cajun seasoning

2 gallons cooking oil, preferably peanut oil

Seasonings and marinades (optional)

1. Fill water tray ⅓ full with 50/50 mixture of apple juice and water. Preheat smoker to 275°F.

2. Rinse and dry thawed turkey. Using a marinade injection syringe, inject turkey with 1 jar (16 ounces) BUTTERBALL® Buttery Creole Marinade. Season outside and inside of turkey with BUTTERBALL® Cajun Seasoning, rubbing it into the skin.

3. Place turkey on middle rack in smoker and close door. Smoke for 2 hours.

4. Remove turkey from smoker, and re-inject with 8 ounces of marinade. Place turkey, breast side up, in fryer basket. Slowly lower basket into hot oil, being careful not to splatter hot oil. Fry turkey for 2 minutes per pound. Lift basket from hot oil slowly. Insert meat thermometer in meaty part of breast; turkey is done when it reads 165°F. If turkey is not done, lower it carefully back into oil for an additional 5 minutes. Once turkey reaches desired temperature (minimum 165°F), remove from oil.

5. Let turkey rest and drain in fryer basket for 10 minutes before removing for carving. Turkey can remain in basket to cool until ready to serve.

6. Based on the weight of your turkey, you will need to adjust the total cooking time, for deep-frying for 2 minutes per pound.

Makes 6 to 12 servings

Additional Seasoning/Marinade Options: We highly recommend the BUTTERBALL® Seasoning Kit with the Buttery Creole Marinade and Cajun Seasoning, but there are other options if you prefer a milder flavor. You can inject the turkey with the marinade of your choice or chicken broth. Season the outside and inside of the turkey with salt and black pepper, rubbing it into the skin. Place 8 to 10 pats of butter underneath the skin. You can also tuck several whole bay leaves underneath the skin.

Baja Fish Tacos

½ cup sour cream

½ cup mayonnaise

¼ cup chopped fresh cilantro

1 packet (1.25 ounces) ORTEGA® Taco Seasoning Mix, divided

1 pound (about 4) cod or other white fish fillets, cut into pieces

2 tablespoons vegetable oil

2 tablespoons lemon juice

1 package (12-count) ORTEGA® Taco Shells, warmed

SUGGESTED TOPPINGS

Shredded cabbage, B&G® Sliced Ripe Olives, lime juice, ORTEGA® Taco Sauce, any variety, chopped tomato

COMBINE sour cream, mayonnaise, cilantro and 2 tablespoons taco seasoning mix in small bowl.

COMBINE cod, vegetable oil, lemon juice and remaining taco seasoning mix in medium bowl; pour into large skillet. Cook, stirring constantly, over medium-high heat for 4 to 5 minutes or until fish flakes easily when tested with fork.

FILL taco shells with fish mixture. Layer with desired toppings. Serve with sour cream sauce.

Makes 12 tacos

TIP

Try a variety of fish and seafood such as shark, shrimp, crab or lobster in these fresh-tasting tacos.

Classic Sloppy Joes

1 tablespoon vegetable oil

½ cup chopped onion

⅓ cup chopped green bell pepper

1 pound lean ground beef

1½ cups HEINZ® Tomato Ketchup

2 tablespoons packed brown sugar

1 tablespoon HEINZ® Worcestershire Sauce

¼ teaspoon salt

¼ teaspoon black pepper

8 sandwich buns

Prep Time: 10 minutes
Cook Time: 25 minutes

1. Heat oil in a large frying pan set over medium-high heat. Cook onion and bell pepper for 5 minutes.

2. Add beef to the pan. Cook, stirring until browned, about 5 to 10 minutes. Drain off fat.

3. Stir in Ketchup, brown sugar, Worcestershire Sauce, salt, and black pepper. Simmer over medium-low heat, stirring occasionally, for 10 minutes or until slightly thickened. Serve on sandwich buns.

Makes 8 servings

Beef Bourguignonne

1 **beef sirloin steak *or* top round steak (about 1 pound), cut into 1-inch pieces**

¼ **cup all-purpose flour**

1 **tablespoon olive oil**

1 **medium onion, chopped (about ½ cup)**

2 **cloves garlic, minced**

⅛ **teaspoon dried parsley flakes**

¼ **teaspoon ground black pepper**

2 **cups sliced mushrooms (about 6 ounces)**

1 **teaspoon dried thyme leaves, crushed**

2 **cups fresh *or* frozen whole baby carrots**

1¾ **cups SWANSON® Beef Stock**

½ **cup Burgundy *or* other dry red wine**

Hot cooked orzo pasta

Prep Time: 10 minutes
Cook Time: 30 minutes

1. Coat the beef with the flour.

2. Heat the oil in a 10-inch skillet over medium-high heat. Add the beef and cook until well browned, stirring often. Add the onion, garlic, parsley, black pepper, mushrooms and thyme and cook until the mushrooms are tender.

3. Stir the carrots, stock and wine in the skillet and heat to a boil. Reduce the heat to low. Cover and cook for 20 minutes or until the beef is cooked through. Serve the beef mixture over the orzo.

Makes 4 servings

Classic Tuna Noodle Casserole

1 can (10¾ ounces)
  CAMPBELL'S® Condensed
  Cream of Celery Soup
  (Regular *or* 98% Fat Free)

½ cup milk

1 cup cooked peas

2 tablespoons chopped
  pimientos

2 cans (about 6 ounces
  each) tuna, drained and
  flaked

2 cups hot cooked medium
  egg noodles

2 tablespoons dry bread
  crumbs

1 tablespoon butter, melted

Prep Time: 10 minutes
Bake Time: 25 minutes

1. Heat the oven to 400°F. Stir the soup, milk, peas, pimientos, tuna and noodles in a 1½-quart baking dish. Stir the bread crumbs and butter in a small bowl.

2. Bake for 20 minutes or until the tuna mixture is hot and bubbling. Stir the tuna mixture. Sprinkle with the bread crumb mixture.

3. Bake for 5 minutes or until the bread crumbs are golden brown.

Makes 4 servings

KITCHEN TIPS

Substitute CAMPBELL'S® Condensed Cream of Mushroom Soup for the Cream of Celery Soup.

To melt the butter, remove the wrapper and place the butter in a microwavable cup. Cover and microwave on HIGH for 30 seconds.

2-Step Inside-Out Chicken Pot Pie

4 **skinless, boneless chicken breast halves (about 1 pound), cut into 1-inch pieces**

1 **can (10¾ ounces) CAMPBELL'S® Condensed Cream of Chicken Soup (Regular _or_ 98% Fat Free)**

1 **bag (16 ounces) frozen vegetable combination (broccoli, cauliflower, carrots)**

8 **hot biscuits, split**

Prep Time: 10 minutes
Cook Time: 15 minutes

1. Cook the chicken in a 10-inch nonstick skillet over medium-high heat until well browned, stirring often.

2. Stir the soup and vegetables in the skillet. Reduce the heat to low. Cover and cook for 5 minutes or until the chicken is cooked through. Serve the chicken and sauce over the biscuits.

Makes 4 servings

Quick Chicken Parmesan

4 skinless, boneless chicken breast halves (about 1 pound)

2 cups PREGO® Traditional Italian Sauce *or* Fresh Mushroom Italian Sauce

2 ounces shredded mozzarella cheese (about ½ cup)

2 tablespoons grated Parmesan cheese

½ of a 16-ounce package spaghetti, cooked and drained (about 4 cups)

Prep Time: 5 minutes
Bake Time: 25 minutes

1. Place the chicken in a 2-quart shallow baking dish. Top the chicken with the Italian sauce. Sprinkle with the mozzarella cheese and Parmesan cheese.

2. Bake at 400°F. for 25 minutes or until cooked through. Serve with the spaghetti.

Makes 4 servings

Take-Two Turkey Tetrazzini

8 ounces dry spaghetti

1 package (16 ounces) frozen vegetable blend (peas, carrots, corn, beans)

1 tablespoon olive oil

¼ cup all-purpose flour

½ teaspoon garlic powder

½ teaspoon salt

½ teaspoon ground black pepper

1 can (14.5 fluid ounces) chicken broth

1 can (12 fluid ounces) NESTLÉ® CARNATION® Evaporated Milk

¾ cup (2¼ ounces) shredded Parmesan cheese, *divided*

2 cups (about 10 ounces) cooked turkey, cut into ½-inch pieces

Prep Time: 20 minutes
Cooking Time: 45 minutes

PREHEAT oven to 350°F. Lightly grease 13×9-inch baking dish.

PREPARE pasta according to package directions, adding frozen vegetables to boiling pasta water for last minute of cooking time; drain. Return pasta and vegetables to cooking pot.

MEANWHILE, HEAT oil in medium saucepan over medium heat. Stir in flour, garlic powder, salt and pepper; cook, stirring constantly, for 1 minute. Remove from heat; gradually stir in broth. Return to heat; bring to boil over medium heat, stirring constantly. Stir in evaporated milk and ½ *cup* cheese; cook over low heat until cheese melts. Remove from heat. Stir in turkey.

POUR cheese sauce over pasta and vegetables; mix lightly. Pour into prepared baking dish. Sprinkle with *remaining ¼ cup* cheese.

BAKE for 20 to 25 minutes or until lightly browned. Serve immediately.

Makes 12 servings

Grilled Italian Sausage & Peppers

1 package (19 ounces)
 JOHNSONVILLE® Italian
 Sausage Links

1 medium sweet red pepper,
 cut into 1-inch pieces

1 medium green pepper,
 cut into 1-inch pieces

1 medium onion, cut into
 1-inch pieces

1 bottle (8 ounces) Italian
 salad dressing

2 cups pasta sauce

10 brat buns, split

20 thin slices provolone
 cheese

1. Cut sausage into ½-inch slices (this works best if partially frozen). In a shallow bowl, combine the sausage, peppers, onion and salad dressing. Cover and refrigerate for 1 hour. Drain and discard marinade.

2. Assemble kabobs on ten metal or soaked wooden skewers, alternately threading sausage, peppers and onion. (Be sure not to make the kabobs longer than the bun.)

3. Grill kabobs over medium heat for 10 to 15 minutes or until vegetables are tender and sausage is no longer pink, turning occasionally.

4. Spread pasta sauce over the inside of buns. Top each with two slices of cheese. Place a kabob inside of each bun. While firmly holding bun against kabob, carefully pull out skewer, leaving sausage and vegetables inside of bun.

Makes 10 servings

Souper Sloppy Joes

1 **pound ground beef**

1 **can (10¾ ounces) CAMPBELL'S® Condensed Tomato Soup**

¼ **cup water**

1 **tablespoon prepared yellow mustard**

6 **PEPPERIDGE FARM® Classic Sandwich Buns with Sesame Seeds**

Prep Time: 5 minutes
Cook Time: 15 minutes

1. Cook the beef in a 10-inch skillet over medium-high heat until well browned, stirring often to separate the meat. Pour off any fat.

2. Stir the soup, water and mustard in the skillet and cook until the mixture is hot and bubbling. Spoon the beef mixture on the buns.

Makes 6 servings

Tasty 2-Step Chicken

1 tablespoon vegetable oil

4 skinless, boneless chicken breast halves (about 1 pound)

1 can (10¾ ounces) CAMPBELL'S® Condensed Cream of Mushroom Soup (Regular, 98% Fat Free *or* Healthy Request®)

½ cup water

Prep Time: 5 minutes
Cook Time: 20 minutes

1. Heat the oil in a 10-inch skillet over medium-high heat. Add the chicken and cook for 10 minutes or until well browned on both sides. Remove the chicken from the skillet.

2. Stir the soup and water in the skillet and heat to a boil. Return the chicken to the skillet. Reduce the heat to low. Cover and cook for 5 minutes or until the chicken is cooked through.

Makes 4 servings

KITCHEN TIP

This recipe is also delicious with CAMPBELL'S® Condensed Cream of Mushroom with Roasted Garlic Soup **or** Cream of Chicken with Herbs Soup.

Roast Turkey with Cornbread-Herb Stuffing

1½ **pounds JENNIE-O TURKEY STORE® Turkey Breast Roast**

1 **tablespoon olive or vegetable oil**

½ **cup each chopped onion and celery**

2 **cups cubed cornbread**

½ **cup finely chopped Canadian bacon**

⅓ **cup chicken broth**

½ **teaspoon each dried sage and crushed thyme**

Salt and pepper

1 **tablespoon margarine or butter**

Dash garlic salt

MUSHROOM GRAVY

1¼ **cups milk**

2 **tablespoons cornstarch**

½ **teaspoon each dried sage and thyme**

1 **can (4 ounces) mushroom stems and pieces, drained**

Salt and pepper

Cook Time: 1 hour

Heat oven to 325°F. In large skillet over medium-high heat, heat oil until hot. Add onion and celery; cook and stir until tender. Remove from heat and stir in cornbread, bacon, broth, sage, thyme and salt and pepper to taste. Cut large pocket in thickest side of turkey. Place turkey in shallow roasting pan. Spoon stuffing into pocket and around turkey. Melt margarine and stir in garlic salt. Brush mixture on turkey. Cover and bake 30 minutes. Uncover and bake until timer pops, 10 to 20 minutes longer. Slice turkey and serve with mushroom gravy.

Makes 4 or 5 servings

Mushroom Gravy: In medium saucepan over high heat, combine milk, cornstarch, sage and thyme. Bring to a boil, stirring constantly, until thickened, about 1 minute. Stir in mushroom stems and pieces and season with salt and pepper to taste. Makes 1¾ cups.

Chicken Noodle Casserole

1 can (10¾ ounces)
CAMPBELL'S® Condensed
Cream of Mushroom
Soup (Regular *or*
98% Fat Free)

½ cup milk

2 tablespoons butter,
melted

¼ teaspoon ground black
pepper

1 cup frozen broccoli
florets, thawed

2 cups shredded cooked
chicken

2 cups hot cooked medium
egg noodles

½ cup grated Parmesan
cheese

Prep Time: 10 minutes
Cook Time: 25 minutes

1. Stir soup, milk, butter, black pepper, broccoli, chicken and noodles in a 2-quart casserole.

2. Bake at 400°F. for 20 minutes or until hot. Stir.

3. Sprinkle with the cheese. Bake for 5 minutes more.

Makes 4 servings

Hot Beef Sandwiches au Jus

4 pounds boneless beef bottom round roast, trimmed*

2 cans (about 10 ounces *each*) condensed beef broth, undiluted

1 can (12 ounces) beer

2 envelopes (1 ounce *each*) dried onion-flavor soup mix

1 tablespoon minced garlic

2 teaspoons sugar

1 teaspoon dried oregano

Crusty French rolls, sliced in half

*Unless you have a 5-, 6- or 7-quart **CROCK-POT®** slow cooker, cut any roast larger than 2½ pounds in half so it cooks completely.

Prep Time: 10 minutes
Cook Time: 6 to 8 hours (HIGH)

1. Place beef in **CROCK-POT®** slow cooker. Combine broth, beer, soup mix, garlic, sugar and oregano in large bowl; stir to blend. Pour mixture over beef. Cover; cook on HIGH 6 to 8 hours.

2. Remove beef to large cutting board; shred with two forks. Return beef to cooking liquid; stir to blend. Serve on rolls with cooking liquid for dipping.

Makes 8 to 10 servings

Double Trouble Tacos

1 **pound ground beef**

1 **ORTEGA® Grande Taco Dinner Kit—includes 12 hard taco shells, 8 flour soft tortillas, 2 packets (3 ounces) taco sauce and 1 packet (2 ounces) taco seasoning mix**

1 **pound cooked chicken breast, shredded**

1 **can (16 ounces) ORTEGA® Refried Beans**

1 **tomato, diced**

2 **cups shredded lettuce**

1 **cup (4 ounces) shredded Cheddar cheese**

Prep Time: 10 minutes
Start to Finish: 25 minutes

BROWN ground beef in large skillet over medium heat 6 to 8 minutes, stirring to break up meat. Drain fat. Add taco seasoning mix from Grande Taco Dinner Kit and ¾ cup water. Mix and set aside.

HEAT chicken in second skillet, adding pouch of taco sauce from Dinner Kit.

SPREAD beans onto flour tortilla. Place yellow corn taco shell inside the flour tortilla. Add ground beef and shredded chicken mixture topped with diced tomatoes, lettuce and cheese.

Makes 8 tacos

TIP

Feel free to replace the ground beef with ground chicken for a Double Trouble Chicken Taco.

Classic Beef and Noodles

1 tablespoon vegetable oil

2 pounds cubed beef stew meat

¼ pound mushrooms, sliced into halves

2 tablespoons chopped onion

2 cloves garlic, minced

1 teaspoon salt

1 teaspoon dried oregano

½ teaspoon black pepper

¼ teaspoon dried marjoram

1 whole bay leaf

1½ cups beef broth

⅓ cup dry sherry

1 container (8 ounces) sour cream

½ cup all-purpose flour

¼ cup water

4 cups hot cooked noodles

Cook Time:
8 to 10 hours (LOW) or
4 to 5 hours (HIGH),
plus 30 minutes

1. Heat oil in large skillet over medium heat. Brown beef in batches on all sides. Drain fat.

2. Combine beef, mushrooms, onion, garlic, salt, oregano, pepper, marjoram and bay leaf in **CROCK-POT**® slow cooker. Pour in broth and sherry. Cover; cook on LOW 8 to 10 hours or on HIGH 4 to 5 hours. Remove and discard bay leaf.

3. Combine sour cream, flour and water in small bowl. Stir about 1 cup cooking liquid from **CROCK-POT**® slow cooker into sour cream mixture. Add mixture to **CROCK-POT**® slow cooker; mix well. Cook, uncovered, on HIGH 30 minutes or until thickened and bubbly. Serve over noodles.

Makes 8 servings

Chicken in Creamy Sun-Dried Tomato Sauce

2 cans (10¾ ounces **each**) CAMPBELL'S® Condensed Cream of Chicken with Herbs Soup **or** CAMPBELL'S® Condensed Cream of Chicken Soup

1 cup Chablis **or** other dry white wine*

¼ cup coarsely chopped pitted kalamata **or** oil-cured olives

2 tablespoons drained capers

2 cloves garlic, minced

1 can (14 ounces) artichoke hearts, drained and chopped

1 cup drained and coarsely chopped sun-dried tomatoes

8 skinless, boneless chicken breast halves (about 2 pounds)

½ cup chopped fresh basil leaves (optional)

Hot cooked rice, egg noodles **or** mashed potatoes

*You can substitute SWANSON® Chicken Broth for the wine, if desired.

Prep Time: 15 minutes
Cook Time: 7 hours

1. Stir the soup, wine, olives, capers, garlic, artichokes and tomatoes in a 3½-quart slow cooker. Add the chicken and turn to coat.

2. Cover and cook on LOW for 7 to 8 hours** or until the chicken is cooked through. Sprinkle with the basil, if desired. Serve with the rice.

**Or on HIGH for 4 to 5 hours.

Makes 8 servings

Italian Sausage Sliders

2 packages (16 ounces each) JOHNSONVILLE® Hot, Mild or Sweet Ground Italian Sausage or 2 packages (19 ounces each) Hot, Mild or Sweet Italian Sausage Links, casings removed*

1 pound ground beef

16 small slider buns or mini sandwich rolls, sliced

Ketchup, mustard, baby greens, sliced cherry tomatoes, roasted red pepper strips, sautéed onions or mushrooms, cheese slices

*Cut sausage link end to end, about three-quarters of the way through; open and flip sausage link over, then grasp casing and pull off.

Prep Time: 10 minutes
Cook Time: 10 minutes

1. Combine sausage and beef in large bowl; mix well. Form into large flat square; cut into quarters, then into 16 small squares. Roll each square into ball and press into patties.

2. Heat large skillet over medium-high heat. Working in batches of four, cook patties about 3 minutes per side or until patties are cooked through (160°F).

3. Place patties on buns and top as desired. Serve immediately.

Makes 16 sliders

Prize-Winning Meatloaf

1½ **pounds 90% lean ground beef**

1 **cup tomato juice or tomato sauce**

¾ **cup QUAKER® Oats (quick or old fashioned, uncooked)**

1 **egg or 2 egg whites, lightly beaten**

¼ **cup chopped onion**

½ **teaspoon salt (optional)**

¼ **teaspoon black pepper**

1. Heat oven to 350°F. Combine beef, tomato juice, oats, egg, onion, salt, if desired, and pepper in large bowl, mixing lightly but thoroughly. Shape into 8×4-inch loaf on rack in broiler pan.

2. Bake 1 hour to medium doneness (160°F) until no longer pink in center and juices show no pink color. Let stand 5 minutes.

Makes 8 servings

Serving Suggestion: Customize meatloaf by adding one of the following: ½ cup frozen (thawed) or canned (drained) corn; ½ cup chopped green or red bell pepper; 1 jar (2½ ounces) sliced mushrooms, drained; ⅓ cup grated Parmesan cheese; 2 tablespoons finely chopped fresh parsley or cilantro.

TIPS

Sprinkle top of baked meatloaf with 1 cup shredded cheese. Return to oven for 3 minutes to melt cheese.

Spoon heated prepared spaghetti sauce, pizza sauce, barbecue sauce or salsa over each serving.

Classic Pot Roast

1 tablespoon vegetable oil

1 boneless beef chuck
   shoulder roast
   (3 to 4 pounds)*

6 medium potatoes, cut into
   halves

6 carrots, sliced

2 medium onions, cut into
   quarters

2 stalks celery, sliced

1 can (about 14 ounces)
   diced tomatoes

   Salt and black pepper

   Dried oregano

2 tablespoons water

1½ to 2 tablespoons
   all-purpose flour

*Unless you have a 5-, 6- or 7-quart
CROCK-POT® slow cooker, cut any roast
larger than 2½ pounds in half so it cooks
completely.

Prep Time: 15 minutes
Cook Time: 8 to 10 hours (LOW)

1. Heat oil in large skillet over medium-low heat. Add roast; cook 6 to 8 minutes or until browned on all sides. Remove to **CROCK-POT**® slow cooker.

2. Add potatoes, carrots, onions, celery and tomatoes. Season with salt, pepper and oregano. Add enough water to cover bottom of **CROCK-POT**® slow cooker by about ½ inch. Cover; cook on LOW 8 to 10 hours.

3. Turn off heat. Remove roast and vegetables to large serving platter using slotted spoon. Let cooking liquid stand 5 minutes. Skim off fat and discard. Turn **CROCK-POT**® slow cooker to HIGH. Stir water into flour in small bowl until smooth; whisk into cooking liquid. Cover; cook on HIGH 10 to 15 minutes or until thickened. Serve sauce over roast and vegetables.

Makes 6 to 8 servings

Melt-in-Your-Mouth Short Ribs

6 serving-sized pieces beef short ribs (about 3 pounds)

2 tablespoons packed brown sugar

3 cloves garlic, minced

1 teaspoon dried thyme leaves, crushed

¼ cup all-purpose flour

1 can (10½ ounces) CAMPBELL'S® Condensed French Onion Soup

1 bottle (12 fluid ounces) dark ale *or* beer

Hot mashed potatoes *or* egg noodles

Prep Time: 10 minutes
Cook Time: 8 hours

1. Place the beef into a 5-quart slow cooker. Add the brown sugar, garlic, thyme and flour and toss to coat.

2. Stir the soup and ale in a small bowl. Pour over the beef.

3. Cover and cook on LOW for 8 to 9 hours* or until the beef is fork-tender. Serve with the mashed potatoes.

*Or on HIGH for 4 to 5 hours.

Makes 6 servings

Corned Beef and Cabbage

2 onions, thickly sliced

1 corned beef brisket (about 3 pounds) with seasoning packet

1 package (8 to 10 ounces) baby carrots

6 medium potatoes, cut into wedges

1 cup water

3 to 5 slices bacon

1 head green cabbage, cut into wedges

1. Place onions in bottom of **CROCK-POT**® slow cooker. Add corned beef with seasoning packet, carrots and potato wedges. Pour 1 cup water over top. Cover; cook on LOW 10 hours.

2. With 30 minutes left in cooking time, heat large saucepan over medium heat. Add bacon; cook and stir until crisp. Remove to paper-towel lined plate using slotted spoon. Reserve drippings in pan. Crumble bacon when cool enough to handle.

3. Place cabbage in saucepan with bacon drippings, cover with water. Bring to a boil; cook 20 to 30 minutes or until cabbage in tender. Drain. Serve corned beef with vegetables; topped with bacon.

Makes 6 servings

Cheesy Chicken & Rice Casserole

1 can (10¾ ounces) **CAMPBELL'S® Condensed Cream of Chicken Soup (Regular, 98% Fat Free** *or* **Healthy Request®)**

1⅓ cups water

¾ cup *uncooked* regular long-grain white rice

½ teaspoon onion powder

¼ teaspoon ground black pepper

2 cups frozen mixed vegetables

4 skinless, boneless chicken breast halves (about 1 pound)

½ cup shredded Cheddar cheese (about 2 ounces)

Bake Time: 50 minutes
Prep Time: 15 minutes
Stand Time: 10 minutes

1. Heat the oven to 375°F. Stir the soup, water, rice, onion powder, black pepper and vegetables in a 2-quart shallow baking dish.

2. Top with the chicken. Cover the baking dish.

3. Bake for 50 minutes or until the chicken is cooked through and the rice is tender. Top with the cheese. Let the casserole stand for 10 minutes. Stir the rice before serving.

Makes 4 servings

Lower Fat: Use CAMPBELL'S® 98% Fat Free Cream of Chicken Soup instead of regular soup and use low-fat cheese instead of regular cheese.

Mexican: In place of the onion powder and black pepper use **1 teaspoon** chili powder. Substitute Mexican cheese blend for the Cheddar.

Italian: In place of the onion powder and black pepper use **1 teaspoon** Italian seasoning, crushed. Substitute ⅓ **cup** shredded Parmesan for the Cheddar.

KITCHEN TIP

To Make Alfredo: Substitute broccoli florets for the vegetables and substitute ¼ **cup** grated Parmesan for the Cheddar cheese. Add **2 tablespoons** Parmesan cheese with the soup. Sprinkle the chicken with the remaining Parmesan cheese.

Slow Cooker Beef & Mushroom Stew

1 **boneless beef bottom round roast** *or* **chuck pot roast (about 1½ pounds), cut into 1-inch pieces**

Ground black pepper

¼ **cup all-purpose flour**

2 **tablespoons vegetable oil**

1 **can (10½ ounces) CAMPBELL'S® Condensed French Onion Soup**

1 **cup Burgundy** *or* **other dry red wine**

2 **cloves garlic, minced**

1 **teaspoon Italian seasoning, crushed**

10 **ounces mushrooms, cut in half (about 3 cups)**

3 **medium carrots, cut into 2-inch pieces (about 1½ cups)**

1 **cup frozen whole small white onions**

¼ **cup water**

Prep Time: 20 minutes
Cook Time: 10 hours 15 minutes

1. Season the beef with the black pepper. Coat the beef with **2 tablespoons** flour. Heat the oil in a 12-inch skillet over medium-high heat. Add the beef and cook until well browned, stirring often.

2. Stir the beef, soup, wine, garlic, Italian seasoning, mushrooms, carrots and onions in a 3½-quart slow cooker.

3. Cover and cook on LOW for 10 to 11 hours* or until the beef is fork-tender.

4. Stir the remaining flour and water in a small bowl until the mixture is smooth. Stir the flour mixture in the cooker. Increase the heat to HIGH. Cover and cook for 15 minutes or until the mixture boils and thickens.

*Or on HIGH for 5 to 6 hours.

Makes 6 servings

Mini Chicken Pot Pies

1 **container (about 16 ounces) refrigerated reduced-fat buttermilk biscuits**

1½ **cups milk**

1 **package (1.8 ounces) white sauce mix**

2 **cups cut-up cooked chicken**

1 **cup frozen assorted vegetables, partially thawed**

2 **cups shredded Cheddar cheese**

2 **cups FRENCH'S® French Fried Onions**

Prep Time: 15 minutes
Cook Time: about 20 minutes

1. Preheat oven to 400°F. Separate biscuits; press into 8 (8-ounce) custard cups, pressing up sides to form crust.

2. Whisk milk and sauce mix in medium saucepan. Bring to boiling over medium-high heat. Reduce heat to medium-low; simmer 1 minute, whisking constantly, until thickened. Stir in chicken and vegetables.

3. Spoon about ⅓ cup chicken mixture into each crust. Place cups on baking sheet. Bake 15 minutes or until golden brown. Top each with cheese and French Fried Onions. Bake 3 minutes or until golden. To serve, remove from cups and transfer to serving plates.

Makes 8 servings

Spicy Bacon Cheeseburger

2 tablespoons FRANK'S®
   RedHot Original
   Cayenne Pepper Sauce

2 tablespoons barbecue
   sauce

1 pound lean ground beef

¼ cup FRENCH'S®
   Worcestershire Sauce

½ teaspoon garlic powder

4 hamburger rolls

4 slices American cheese

4 cooked bacon strips

Prep Time: 10 minutes
Cook Time: 15 minutes

COMBINE **FRANK'S RedHot** Original Cayenne Pepper
Sauce and barbecue sauce; set aside.

MIX beef, Worcestershire sauce and garlic powder;
shape into 4 burgers.

GRILL over medium heat 15 minutes or until cooked
through, turning once.

PLACE burgers on rolls. Top *each* with a slice of cheese,
1 tablespoon **FRANK'S RedHot** mixture and *1* piece
bacon.

Makes 4 servings

Best Ever Meatloaf

2 pounds ground beef

1 can (10¾ ounces) CAMPBELL'S® Condensed Tomato Soup (Regular *or* Healthy Request®)

1 envelope (about 1 ounce) dry onion soup and recipe mix

½ cup dry bread crumbs

1 egg, beaten

¼ cup water

Prep Time: 10 minutes
Bake Time: 1 hour 15 minutes
Stand Time: 10 minutes
Cook Time: 5 minutes

1. Thoroughly mix the beef, ½ **cup** tomato soup, onion soup mix, bread crumbs and egg in a large bowl. Place the mixture into a 13×9×2-inch baking pan and firmly shape into an 8×4-inch loaf.

2. Bake at 350°F. for 1 hour 15 minutes or until the meatloaf is cooked through. Let the meatloaf stand for 10 minutes before slicing.

3. Heat **2 tablespoons** pan drippings, remaining tomato soup and water in a 1-quart saucepan over medium heat until the mixture is hot and bubbling. Serve the sauce with the meatloaf.

Makes 8 servings

KITCHEN TIP

You can substitute CAMPBELL'S® Condensed Cream of Mushroom Soup (Regular **or** 98% Fat Free) for the Tomato Soup.

Easy Chicken & Cheese Enchiladas

1 can (10¾ ounces)
  CAMPBELL'S® Condensed
  Cream of Chicken Soup
  (Regular *or* 98% Fat Free)

½ cup sour cream

1 cup PACE® Picante Sauce

2 teaspoons chili powder

2 cups chopped cooked
  chicken

½ cup shredded Monterey
  Jack cheese

6 flour tortillas (6-inch),
  warmed

1 small tomato, chopped
  (about ½ cup)

1 green onion, sliced (about
  2 tablespoons)

Prep Time: 15 minutes
Bake Time: 40 minutes

1. Heat the oven to 350°F. Stir the soup, sour cream, picante sauce and chili powder in a medium bowl.

2. Stir **1 cup** soup mixture, chicken and cheese in a large bowl.

3. Divide the chicken mixture among the tortillas. Roll up the tortillas and place seam-side up in a 2-quart shallow baking dish. Pour the remaining soup mixture over the filled tortillas. **Cover** the baking dish.

4. Bake for 40 minutes or until the enchiladas are hot and bubbling. Top with the tomato and onion.

Makes 6 servings

KITCHEN TIP

Stir ½ **cup** canned black beans, rinsed and drained, into the chicken mixture before filling the tortillas.

Slow-Cooked Pulled Pork Sandwiches

1 tablespoon vegetable oil

1 boneless pork shoulder roast (3½ to 4 pounds), netted or tied

1 can (10½ ounces) CAMPBELL'S® Condensed French Onion Soup

1 cup ketchup

¼ cup cider vinegar

3 tablespoons packed brown sugar

12 PEPPERIDGE FARM® Sandwich Buns

Prep Time: 15 minutes
Cook Time: 8 hours
Stand Time: 10 minutes

1. Heat the oil in a 10-inch skillet over medium-high heat. Add the pork and cook until well browned on all sides.

2. Stir the soup, ketchup, vinegar and brown sugar in a 5-quart slow cooker. Add the pork and turn to coat.

3. Cover and cook on LOW for 8 to 9 hours* or until the pork is fork-tender.

4. Remove the pork from the cooker to a cutting board and let stand for 10 minutes. Using 2 forks, shred the pork. Return the pork to the cooker.

5. Spoon the pork and sauce mixture on the buns.

Makes 12 servings

RAGÚ® No Frying Chicken Parmesan

¾ **cup plain dry bread crumbs**

½ **teaspoon Italian seasoning**

¼ **teaspoon garlic powder**

6 **boneless, skinless chicken breast halves**

1 **egg, beaten**

1 **jar (1 pound 8 ounces) RAGÚ® Old World Style® Pasta Sauce**

1 **cup shredded part-skim mozzarella cheese (about 4 ounces)**

Prep Time: 20 minutes
Cook Time: 30 minutes

1. Preheat oven to 400°F. Combine bread crumbs, Italian seasoning and garlic powder in shallow dish. Dip chicken in egg, then crumbs mixture; turn to coat.

2. Arrange chicken in 13×9-inch baking dish. Bake 20 minutes.

3. Pour Pasta Sauce over chicken; top with cheese. Bake an additional 10 minutes or until chicken is thoroughly cooked.

Makes 6 servings

No Frying Eggplant Parmesan

2 cups plain dry bread crumbs

1½ cups grated Parmesan cheese, divided

½ teaspoon Italian seasoning

¼ teaspoon garlic powder

2 medium eggplants (about 2 pounds), peeled and cut into ¼-inch slices

4 eggs, beaten with 3 tablespoons water

1 jar (1 pound 10 ounces) RAGÚ® ROBUSTO!® Pasta Sauce

1½ cups shredded part-skim mozzarella cheese (about 6 ounces)

Prep Time: 10 minutes
Cook Time: 1 hour 20 minutes

1. Preheat oven to 350°F. Combine bread crumbs with ½ cup Parmesan cheese, Italian seasoning and garlic powder in medium bowl. Dip eggplant slices in egg mixture, then bread crumb mixture. Arrange eggplant slices in single layer on lightly oiled baking sheets. Bake 25 minutes or until eggplant is golden.

2. Evenly spread 1 cup RAGÚ® ROBUSTO!® Pasta Sauce in 13×9-inch baking dish. Layer ½ of the baked eggplant slices, then 1 cup Sauce and ½ cup Parmesan cheese; repeat layers. Cover with aluminum foil and bake 45 minutes. Remove foil and sprinkle with mozzarella cheese. Bake, uncovered, an additional 10 minutes or until cheese is melted.

Makes 6 servings

 TIP

Get your kids to eat more veggies by letting them help. Breading the eggplant slices is a great way to make veggies fun.

Broccoli Fish Bake

1 package (about 10 ounces) frozen broccoli spears, cooked and drained

4 fresh or thawed frozen firm white fish fillets (cod, haddock *or* halibut) (about 1 pound)

1 can (10¾ ounces) CAMPBELL'S® Condensed Cream of Broccoli Soup

⅓ cup milk

¼ cup shredded Cheddar cheese

2 tablespoons dry bread crumbs

1 teaspoon butter, melted

⅛ teaspoon paprika

Prep Time: 15 minutes
Bake Time: 20 minutes

1. Place the broccoli into a 2-quart shallow baking dish. Top with the fish. Stir the soup and milk in a small bowl. Pour the soup mixture over the fish. Sprinkle with the cheese.

2. Stir the bread crumbs, butter and paprika in a small bowl. Sprinkle the crumb mixture over all.

3. Bake at 450°F. for 20 minutes or until the fish flakes easily when tested with a fork.

Makes 4 servings

KITCHEN TIP

You can substitute **1 pound** fresh broccoli spears, cooked and drained, for the frozen.

Turkey Piccata

1 lemon

1 tablespoon olive oil

4 turkey breast cutlets *or* slices

1 medium onion, chopped (about ½ cup)

1 can (10¾ ounces) CAMPBELL'S® Condensed Cream of Chicken Soup (Regular *or* 98% Fat Free)

½ cup milk

2 tablespoons cooked crumbled bacon

Hot cooked rice

Prep Time: 5 minutes
Cook Time: 20 minutes

1. Cut **4** thin slices of lemon. Squeeze **2 teaspoons** juice from the remaining lemon. Set aside.

2. Heat the oil in a 12-inch skillet over medium-high heat. Add the turkey in 2 batches and cook for 3 minutes or until the turkey is lightly browned on both sides. Remove the turkey.

3. Add the onion and cook until tender.

4. Stir the soup, milk and reserved lemon juice into the skillet. Heat to a boil. Return the turkey to the skillet and reduce the heat to low. Top the turkey with the lemon slices. Cover and cook for 5 minutes or until the turkey is cooked through. Sprinkle with the bacon. Serve with rice.

Makes 4 servings

KITCHEN TIP

For the amount of bacon needed, use **1 slice** bacon, cooked and crumbled or bacon bits.

Barbecued Turkey Burgers

- **1** package **JENNIE-O TURKEY STORE® Ground Turkey**
- **¼** cup prepared **barbecue sauce**
- **2** tablespoons dry **bread crumbs**
- **4** whole grain sandwich **buns**

CLASSIC COLESLAW

- **2** cups thinly shredded **cabbage**
- **¼** cup each shredded carrot **and thinly sliced red onion**
- **3** tablespoons reduced-**calorie mayonnaise**
- **2** teaspoons each lime juice **and granulated sugar**

Cook Time: 15 minutes

In medium bowl, combine turkey, barbecue sauce and bread crumbs; mix lightly. Shape into 4 patties (½ inch thick). Grill over hot coals, 4 inches from heat, until meat springs back when touched and burgers are no longer pink in center, about 4 minutes per side. Serve burgers topped with Classic Coleslaw in buns.

Makes 4 servings

Classic Coleslaw: In large bowl, combine cabbage, carrot, onion, mayonnaise, lime juice and sugar. Mix well. Makes about 2½ cups.

Sloppy Joe Casserole

1 **pound ground beef**

1 **can (10¾ ounces)
CAMPBELL'S®
Condensed Tomato Soup
(Regular *or* Healthy
Request®)**

¼ **cup water**

1 **teaspoon Worcestershire
sauce**

⅛ **teaspoon ground black
pepper**

1 **package (7.5 ounces)
refrigerated biscuits
(10 biscuits)**

½ **cup shredded Cheddar
cheese (about 2 ounces)**

Prep Time: 15 minutes
Bake Time: 15 minutes

1. Heat the oven to 400°F.

2. Cook the beef in a 10-inch skillet over medium-high heat until well browned, stirring often to separate the meat. Pour off any fat.

3. Stir the soup, water, Worcestershire and black pepper in the skillet and heat to a boil. Spoon the beef mixture into a 1½-quart casserole. Arrange the biscuits around the inside edge of the casserole.

4. Bake for 15 minutes or until the biscuits are golden brown. Sprinkle the cheese over the beef mixture.

Makes 5 servings

KITCHEN TIP
Sharp **or** mild Cheddar cheese will work in this recipe.

Chicken & Broccoli Alfredo

½ **of a 16-ounce package linguine**

1 **cup fresh** *or* **frozen broccoli florets**

2 **tablespoons butter**

4 **skinless, boneless chicken breast halves (about 1 pound), cut into 1½-inch pieces**

1 **can (10¾ ounces) CAMPBELL'S® Condensed Cream of Mushroom Soup (Regular, 98% Fat Free** *or* **Healthy Request®)**

½ **cup milk**

½ **cup grated Parmesan cheese**

¼ **teaspoon ground black pepper**

Prep Time: 10 minutes
Cook Time: 20 minutes

KITCHEN TIP

You can substitute spaghetti **or** fettuccine for the linguine in this recipe.

1. Prepare the linguine according to the package directions in a 3-quart saucepan. Add the broccoli during the last 4 minutes of the cooking time. Drain the linguine mixture well in a colander.

2. Heat the butter in a 10-inch skillet over medium-high heat. Add the chicken and cook until well browned, stirring often.

3. Stir the soup, milk, cheese, black pepper and linguine mixture in the skillet and cook until the chicken is cooked through, stirring occasionally. Serve with additional Parmesan cheese.

Makes 4 servings

Grilled Chicken & Broccoli Alfredo: Substitute grilled chicken breasts for the skinless, boneless chicken.

Shrimp & Broccoli Alfredo: Substitute **1 pound** fresh extra large shrimp, peeled and deveined, for the chicken. Cook as directed for the chicken above, until the shrimp are cooked through.

Spanish-Inspired Tip: Reduce the chicken to ½ **pound** and omit the Parmesan cheese. Prepare as directed above. Stir ½ **pound** peeled cooked shrimp, ¼ **pound** chorizo **or** ham, diced, and **1 teaspoon** paprika into the soup mixture.

Indian-Inspired Tip: Omit the Parmesan cheese. Substitute **3 cups** cooked basmati rice and ¾ **cup** cooked broccoli florets for the linguine and **uncooked** broccoli. Stir **1 teaspoon** curry powder and ½ **teaspoon** ground cumin into the skillet with the chicken. Sprinkle with toasted slivered almonds, if desired.

Asian-Inspired Tip: Omit the Parmesan cheese. Substitute **1 package** (6 ounces) rice noodles for the linguine. Prepare as directed above. Stir **1 tablespoon** soy sauce, **2** cloves garlic, minced, and **2 teaspoons** minced fresh ginger root in the skillet and cook with the chicken.

Hearty Chicken & Noodle Casserole

1 **can (10¾ ounces)
CAMPBELL'S® Condensed
Cream of Mushroom Soup
(Regular *or* 98% Fat Free)**

½ **cup milk**

1 **cup frozen mixed
vegetables**

2 **cups cubed cooked chicken**

2 **cups medium egg noodles,
cooked and drained**

¼ **cup grated Parmesan
cheese**

¼ **teaspoon ground black
pepper**

½ **cup shredded Cheddar
cheese (about 2 ounces)**

Prep Time: 15 minutes
Bake Time: 25 minutes

1. Heat the oven to 400°F. Stir the soup, milk, vegetables, chicken, noodles, Parmesan cheese and black pepper in a 1½-quart casserole.

2. Bake for 25 minutes or until the chicken mixture is hot and bubbling. Stir the chicken mixture. Top with the Cheddar cheese. Let stand until the cheese is melted.

Makes 4 servings

KITCHEN TIP

Easy casseroles like this one are a simple way to transform leftovers. Cooked chicken, turkey **or** ham will all work in this recipe.

Savory Pot Roast

2 tablespoons vegetable oil

1 boneless beef bottom round roast *or* chuck pot roast (3½ to 4 pounds)

1 can (10¾ ounces) CAMPBELL'S® Condensed Cream of Mushroom Soup (Regular *or* 98% Fat Free)

1¼ cups water

1 envelope (about 1 ounce) dry onion soup and recipe mix

6 medium potatoes, cut into quarters

6 medium carrots, cut into 2-inch pieces (about 3 cups)

2 tablespoons all-purpose flour

Prep Time: 15 minutes
Cook Time: 2 hours 50 minutes

1. Heat the oil in a 6-quart saucepot over medium-high heat. Add the beef and cook until well browned on all sides. Pour off any fat.

2. Stir the mushroom soup, **1 cup** water and soup mix in a medium bowl. Add the soup mixture to the saucepot and heat to a boil. Reduce the heat to low. Cover and cook for 1 hour 30 minutes.

3. Add the potatoes and carrots to the saucepot. Cover and cook for 1 hour or until the beef is fork-tender and the vegetables are tender. Remove the beef and vegetables to a serving platter.

4. Stir the flour and remaining water in a small bowl until the mixture is smooth. Stir the flour mixture in the saucepot. Cook and stir until the mixture boils and thickens. Serve the gravy with the beef and vegetables.

Makes 8 servings

Barbecued Pulled Pork Sandwiches

1 pork shoulder roast
   (2½ pounds)

1 bottle (14 ounces)
   barbecue sauce

1 tablespoon lemon juice

1 teaspoon packed brown
   sugar

1 medium onion, chopped

8 hamburger buns

Prep Time: 15 to 20 minutes
Cook Time:
11 to 13 hours (LOW) or
6 to 7 hours (HIGH)
plus 30 minutes

1. Place pork in **CROCK-POT**® slow cooker. Cover; cook on LOW 10 to 12 hours or on HIGH 5 to 6 hours.

2. Remove pork to large cutting board; shred with two forks. Discard cooking liquid. Return pork to **CROCK-POT**® slow cooker. Add barbecue sauce, lemon juice, brown sugar and onion. Cover; cook on LOW 2 hours or on HIGH 1 hour. Serve on buns.

Makes 8 servings

Serving Suggestion: Serve with coleslaw.

TIP

For a 5-, 6- or 7-quart **CROCK-POT**® slow cooker, double all ingredients except for the barbecue sauce. Increase the barbecue sauce to 1½ bottles (about 21 ounces total).

Baked Ziti Supreme

1 **pound ground beef**

1 **medium onion, chopped (about ½ cup)**

1 **jar (24 ounces) PREGO® Fresh Mushroom Italian Sauce**

1½ **cups shredded mozzarella cheese (6 ounces)**

5 **cups medium tube-shaped pasta (ziti), cooked and drained**

¼ **cup grated Parmesan cheese**

Prep Time: 25 minutes
Bake Time: 30 minutes

1. Cook the beef and onion in a 4-quart saucepan over medium-high heat until the beef is well browned, stirring often to separate the meat. Pour off any fat.

2. Stir the Italian sauce, **1 cup** mozzarella cheese and pasta in the saucepan. Spoon the mixture into a 3-quart shallow baking dish. Sprinkle with the remaining mozzarella cheese and Parmesan cheese. Bake at 350°F. for 30 minutes or until hot and bubbling.

Makes 6 servings

Korean Soft Tacos

¼ **cup granulated sugar**

¼ **cup rice wine vinegar**

2 **tablespoons soy sauce**

1 **ORTEGA® Soft Taco Kit—
includes 10 flour soft
tortillas, 1 packet
(1.25 ounces) taco
seasoning mix and
1 packet (3 ounces) taco
sauce**

2 **pounds thin-sliced rib-eye
steaks**

2 **cups bean sprouts**

1 **red bell pepper, cut into
strips**

1 **yellow bell pepper, cut into
strips**

6 **green onions, diced**

2 **tablespoons sesame oil**

2 **limes, cut into wedges**

Prep Time: 10 minutes
Start to Finish: 2 hours 20 minutes

COMBINE sugar, vinegar, soy sauce and taco sauce from Taco Kit in medium bowl. Add steaks; toss gently to coat with marinade. Cover; marinate in refrigerator 2 hours.

COMBINE bean sprouts, bell peppers and green onions in medium bowl. Sprinkle with seasoning mix from Taco Kit; toss gently. Set aside.

REMOVE steaks from marinade; slice into long strips. Reserve any marinade.

HEAT sesame oil in large skillet over medium heat. Add steak strips and sear lightly. Add 2 to 3 tablespoons remaining marinade mixture; cook and stir 3 to 4 minutes or until steak is cooked to desired doneness. Discard remaining marinade.

WRAP tortillas from Taco Kit with a clean, lightly moistened cloth or paper towels. Microwave on HIGH (100% power) 1 minute, or until hot and pliable.

DIVIDE beef mixture evenly among tortillas. Garnish with taco-seasoned vegetables. Serve with lime wedges.

Makes 10 tacos

TIP
For an authentic taste of Mexican street food, garnish with fresh cilantro.

Pasta & Pizza

Shortcut Ravioli Lasagna

Vegetable cooking spray

3 cups PREGO® Italian Sausage & Garlic Italian Sauce

½ cup water

1 package (30 ounces) frozen regular-size cheese-filled ravioli (about 30 to 34)

6 ounces shredded mozzarella cheese (about 1½ cups)

Grated Parmesan cheese and chopped fresh parsley for garnish

Prep Time: 10 minutes
Bake Time: 45 minutes
Stand Time: 10 minutes

1. Heat the oven to 375°F. Spray a 13×9×2-inch baking dish with cooking spray.

2. Stir the Italian sauce and water in a large bowl. Spread **1 cup** of the Italian sauce mixture in the baking dish. Top with ½ of the ravioli, ¾ **cup** mozzarella cheese and **1 cup** sauce mixture. Top with the remaining ravioli and sauce mixture. Cover the baking dish.

3. Bake for 35 minutes or until the mixture is hot and bubbling. Uncover the baking dish. Sprinkle with the remaining mozzarella cheese.

4. Bake for 10 minutes or until the cheese is melted. Let stand for 10 minutes. Garnish with the Parmesan cheese and parsley.

Makes 6 servings

Pizza Margherita

1 cup BERTOLLI® Tomato & Basil Sauce

1 (12-inch) prebaked pizza crust

4 ounces fresh mozzarella cheese, thinly sliced

1 tablespoon BERTOLLI® CLASSICO™ Olive Oil

¼ cup chopped fresh basil leaves

Prep Time: 5 minutes
Cook Time: 10 minutes

1. Preheat oven to 450°F.

2. Evenly spread BERTOLLI® Tomato & Basil Sauce on pizza crust, then top with cheese. Bake 10 minutes or until cheese is melted.

3. Drizzle with BERTOLLI® CLASSICO™ Olive Oil, sprinkle with basil and serve immediately.

Makes 4 servings

2-Step Cheesy Pasta Twists

6 cups corkscrew-shaped pasta (rotini), cooked and drained

1 jar (24 ounces) **PREGO®** Traditional Italian Sauce *or* Italian Sausage & Garlic Italian Sauce

1 cup shredded mozzarella cheese (about 4 ounces)

½ cup **PEPPERIDGE FARM®** Zesty Italian Croutons, crushed

Prep Time: 20 minutes
Cook Time: 10 minutes

1. Stir the pasta and Italian sauce in a 10-inch skillet and heat over medium heat until the mixture is hot and bubbling.

2. Reduce the heat to low. Top with cheese and crushed croutons. Cover and cook until the cheese is melted.

Makes 4 servings

Classic Macaroni and Cheese

- **2 cups elbow macaroni, cooked and drained**
- **3 tablespoons butter or margarine**
- **¼ cup finely chopped onion (optional)**
- **2 tablespoons all-purpose flour**
- **½ teaspoon salt**
- **⅛ teaspoon black pepper**
- **2 cups milk**
- **2 cups (8 ounces) SARGENTO® Fine Cut Shredded Mild Cheddar Cheese, divided**

Prep Time: 15 minutes
Cook Time: 30 minutes

1. Melt butter in medium saucepan over medium heat. Cook onion, if desired, in butter 5 minutes or until tender. Stir in flour, salt and pepper. Gradually add milk and cook, stirring occasionally, until thickened.

2. Remove from heat. Add 1½ cups cheese and stir until cheese is melted. Combine cheese sauce with cooked macaroni. Place in 1½-quart casserole; top with remaining cheese. Bake in preheated 350°F oven 30 minutes or until bubbly and cheese is lightly browned.

Makes 6 servings

Creamy Vegetable Lasagna

1 tablespoon olive oil

2 medium zucchini, cut lengthwise into quarters, then into ½-inch pieces

2 medium bell peppers (red, green or yellow), chopped into ½-inch pieces

2 garlic cloves, finely chopped

½ teaspoon salt, *divided*

½ teaspoon ground black pepper, *divided*

⅓ cup all-purpose flour

2 cans (12 fluid ounces *each*) NESTLÉ® CARNATION® Evaporated Lowfat 2% Milk, *divided*

1 jar (26 ounces) prepared marinara sauce, *divided*

1 package (8 ounces) or 12 sheets no-boil lasagna noodles, *divided*

1½ cups (6 ounces) shredded part-skim mozzarella cheese, *divided*

½ cup grated Parmesan cheese (optional)

PREHEAT oven to 375°F. Grease 13×9-inch baking dish.

HEAT oil in large skillet over medium-high heat. Add zucchini and peppers; cook, stirring frequently, until soft, for about 8 minutes. Add garlic; cook for an additional 2 minutes. Season with *¼ teaspoon* each salt and pepper. Remove from heat.

MEANWHILE, WHISK together flour, *¼ cup* evaporated milk and *remaining ¼ teaspoon* each of salt and black pepper in medium saucepan until smooth. Whisk in *remaining* evaporated milk. Heat over medium heat, stirring frequently, until mixture comes to a boil. Reduce heat; simmer for 3 minutes or until thickened. Stir *2 cups* of milk mixture into cooked vegetables; reserve *remaining* milk mixture.

SPREAD *½ cup* marinara sauce over bottom of the prepared baking dish. Top with 3 noodles. Top with *half* of the vegetable mixture. Top with 3 noodles. Spread *1 cup* marinara sauce and sprinkle with *¾ cup* mozzarella cheese. Layer 3 noodles, *remaining* vegetables and *remaining* 3 noodles. Top with *remaining* marinara sauce, reserved milk mixture, *remaining ¾ cup* mozzarella cheese and Parmesan cheese.

BAKE for 35 to 40 minutes until golden and bubbly on the edges. Let stand for 10 minutes before serving.

Makes 12 servings

TIP

For extra flavor, add a bay leaf to the white sauce while cooking.

Stuffed Spinach Pizza

1 loaf (1 pound) frozen white bread dough

1½ cups chopped plum tomatoes

½ pound bulk Italian sausage, cooked and well drained (optional)

1 teaspoon dried basil

¼ teaspoon dried oregano

¼ teaspoon pepper

2 cups (15 ounces) SARGENTO® Whole Milk Ricotta Cheese

½ package (10 ounces) frozen chopped spinach, thawed and squeezed dry

1 cup (4 ounces) SARGENTO® Fine Cut Shredded Mozzarella Cheese

1 cup (4 ounces) SARGENTO® ARTISAN BLENDS® Shredded Parmesan Cheese, divided

1 clove garlic, minced

¼ teaspoon salt

½ cup pizza sauce

Prep Time: 15 minutes
Cook Time: 35 minutes

1. Thaw bread dough and let rise according to package directions. Roll two-thirds dough into 11-inch circle on lightly floured surface. Line bottom and sides of greased 9-inch cake pan with dough. Place tomatoes and sausage, if desired, in pan; sprinkle with basil, oregano and pepper.

2. Combine Ricotta, spinach, Mozzarella cheese, ¾ cup Parmesan cheese, garlic and salt in small bowl; spread over tomatoes. Roll remaining dough into 9-inch circle; place over cheese mixture. Pinch edges to seal. Bake in preheated 450°F oven 25 minutes. Spread with pizza sauce; sprinkle with remaining Parmesan cheese. Bake additional 10 minutes. Let stand 10 minutes before serving.

Makes 8 servings

Chicken Parmesan Pasta Toss

1 jar (1 pound 8 ounces) RAGÚ® Old World Style® Pasta Sauce or RAGÚ® Organic Pasta Sauce

8 ounces fusilli, bucati or your favorite pasta, cooked and drained

1 package (12 ounces) baked breaded low fat chicken breast tenders, heated according to package directions

2 cups shredded mozzarella cheese (about 8 ounces)

Prep Time: 20 minutes
Cook Time: 5 minutes

1. Heat Pasta Sauce in 2-quart saucepan.

2. Combine hot Sauce, pasta, chicken and 1 cup cheese in large serving bowl. Top with remaining 1 cup cheese and serve immediately.

Makes 4 servings

Lasagne Authentico

1 recipe Classic Tomato
Sauce (recipe below) or
1 jar (30 ounces) pasta
sauce

1 pound ground beef, cooked
and drained

4 cups (30 ounces)
SARGENTO® Whole Milk
Ricotta Cheese

1½ cups (6 ounces)
SARGENTO® ARTISAN
BLENDS® Shredded
Parmesan Cheese, divided

3 tablespoons minced fresh
parsley

½ pound lasagna noodles,
cooked and drained

3 cups (12 ounces)
SARGENTO® Traditional
Cut Shredded Mozzarella
Cheese

CLASSIC TOMATO SAUCE

2 cans (28 ounces each)
Italian tomatoes

1 carrot, chopped

1 medium onion, chopped

¼ cup olive oil

4 cloves garlic, minced

1 can (6 ounces) tomato
paste

¼ cup dry red wine

¼ cup minced fresh parsley

1 tablespoon dried basil,
crushed

1 tablespoon dried oregano,
crushed

1 teaspoon salt

½ teaspoon black pepper

1. In medium bowl, combine tomato sauce and ground beef. In a separate medium bowl, combine Ricotta cheese, ¾ cup Parmesan cheese and parsley.

2. Pour ¾ cup tomato mixture in bottom of 13×9-inch pan. Layer one-third noodles, half the Ricotta mixture, one-third of the remaining tomato sauce and 1 cup Mozzarella cheese in pan. Repeat layers. Top with remaining noodles, tomato sauce and 1 cup Mozzarella and ¾ cup Parmesan cheeses.

3. Cover with foil and bake at 350°F 50 minutes; uncover and bake 15 minutes more. Let stand 10 minutes before serving.

Makes 12 servings

FOR CLASSIC TOMATO SAUCE: Drain tomatoes, reserve juice. Finely chop tomatoes; set aside. In large saucepan, cook carrot and onion in olive oil until tender. Add garlic; cook 1 minute. Add reserved juice, tomatoes, tomato paste, red wine, parsley, basil, oregano, salt and pepper. Simmer 1 hour, stirring occasionally.

Prep Time: 60 minutes
Cook Time: 65 minutes

Chicken Garden Pasta

6 oz. (2 cups) dried rotini or penne pasta

2 skinless, boneless chicken breast halves, cut in strips

Garlic powder, salt and pepper (optional)

1 cup sliced green or yellow sweet pepper

½ medium onion, thinly sliced

1 Tbsp. olive oil

1 can (14.5 oz.) DEL MONTE® Diced Tomatoes with Basil, Garlic and Oregano

Olives (optional)

Parmesan cheese (optional)

Prep Time: 10 minutes
Cook Time: 40 minutes

1. Cook pasta according to package directions; drain.

2. Meanwhile, season chicken with garlic powder, salt and pepper, if desired.

3. Cook chicken, sweet pepper and onion in oil in large skillet over medium-high heat 5 minutes or until chicken is no longer pink.

4. Add undrained tomatoes; simmer, uncovered, 5 minutes or until slightly thickened. Add olives, if desired. Season with garlic powder, salt and pepper, if desired.

5. Toss with hot pasta. Serve with shredded Parmesan cheese.

Makes 4 servings

Mama's Best Ever Spaghetti & Meatballs

1 **pound lean ground beef**

½ **cup Italian seasoned dry bread crumbs**

1 **egg**

1 **jar (1 pound 8 ounces) RAGÚ® OLD WORLD STYLE® Pasta Sauce**

8 **ounces spaghetti, cooked and drained**

Prep Time: 20 minutes
Cook Time: 20 minutes

1. Combine ground beef, bread crumbs and egg in medium bowl; shape into 12 meatballs.

2. Bring RAGÚ® OLD WORLD STYLE® Pasta Sauce to a boil over medium-high heat in 3-quart saucepan. Gently stir in uncooked meatballs. Reduce heat to low and simmer covered, stirring occasionally, 20 minutes or until meatballs are done.

3. Serve over hot spaghetti and garnish, if desired, with grated Parmesan cheese.

Makes 4 servings

Variation: Try adding a cube of mozzarella cheese to the center of each meatball for an easy but fun recipe twist.

Tomatoes Tricolor Grilled Pizza

1 **10 to 12-inch pre-baked pizza crust**

2 **tablespoons olive oil**

¾ **cup spicy marinara sauce**

1 **tablespoon minced garlic**

2 **cups (8 ounces) SARGENTO® ARTISAN BLENDS® Shredded Whole Milk Mozzarella & Provolone Cheese, divided**

3 **medium tomatoes (1 red, 1 yellow, 1 orange), sliced**

10 **torn fresh basil leaves**

10 **arugula leaves**

Prep Time: 10 minutes
Cook Time: 8 minutes

1. Preheat grill to medium to medium-high heat.

2. Place foil on cookie sheet or wooden pizza paddle; top with crust. Brush crust with olive oil. Spread sauce over crust; sprinkle with garlic and 1 cup cheese. Top with tomatoes.

3. Sprinkle remaining cheese over pizza. Transfer pizza, still on foil, to top of grill. Grill pizza, covered, 3 to 4 minutes. Uncover and grill 3 to 4 minutes more, until the crust browns on the bottom and the cheese melts. Top with basil and arugula leaves. Remove from grill and serve.

Makes 4 servings

JOHNSONVILLE® All Natural Ground Italian Sausage Lasagna

12 lasagna noodles,
   uncooked

1 package (16 ounces)
   JOHNSONVILLE® Ground
   Italian Sausage

1 medium onion, chopped

1 tablespoon chopped
   garlic

1 large container of chunky
   pasta sauce

1 container (15 ounces)
   ricotta cheese

1 egg

⅔ cup grated Parmesan
   cheese, divided

3 cups packed chopped
   fresh spinach

2 cups shredded mozzarella
   cheese

Prep Time: 20 minutes
Cook Time: 45 minutes

1. Prepare noodles according to package directions; drain and set aside. Sauté Italian sausage, onion and garlic in a skillet until sausage is browned; drain. Add pasta sauce to the sausage mixture and set aside. In a medium bowl, blend ricotta cheese, egg and ¼ cup of Parmesan cheese and set aside.

2. Preheat oven to 350°F. Coat a 13×9-inch baking dish with nonstick spray and spread 1 cup of the sauce mixture on the bottom. Top with 3 lasagna noodles. Spread ¼ cup of the ricotta cheese mixture on the noodles and layer on 1 cup of the sauce mixture. Sprinkle 1 cup of the spinach and ½ cup mozzarella cheese. Repeat layers 3 more times starting with the noodles; top with remaining Parmesan cheese.

3. Bake, uncovered, for 45 minutes until hot and bubbly. Let stand 10 minutes before cutting.

Makes 12 servings

Cheese and Fresh Vegetable Pizza

1 can (10 ounces) refrigerated pizza dough

½ cup thinly sliced red onion

2 cloves garlic, minced

1 small green or red bell pepper, cut into 1-inch strips

½ cup (4 ounces) sliced fresh mushrooms

1½ cups (6 ounces) SARGENTO® Shredded Reduced Fat Mozzarella Cheese, divided

4 plum tomatoes, sliced

1 teaspoon dried basil

½ teaspoon dried oregano

Prep Time: 15 minutes
Cook Time: 16 minutes

1. Spray 12-inch pizza pan with nonstick cooking spray. Unroll crust; press onto prepared pan. Bake in preheated 425°F oven 6 minutes or until crust is just beginning to brown.

2. Spray skillet with nonstick cooking spray; stir in onion and garlic. Cook over medium heat 2 minutes until onion is soft. Add bell pepper and mushrooms; cook 2 minutes. Remove from heat; set aside.

3. Sprinkle ¾ cup cheese over crust. Arrange tomato slices over cheese; sprinkle with basil and oregano. Top with mushroom mixture and remaining cheese. Bake in preheated 425°F oven 10 minutes or until crust is crisp and cheese is melted.

Makes 6 servings

Two Cheese Macaroni Bake

2 tablespoons butter

2½ tablespoons all-purpose flour

2 cups milk

¾ teaspoon salt

⅛ teaspoon cayenne pepper

8 ounces elbow macaroni, mostaccioli or penne pasta, cooked and drained

4 slices SARGENTO® Deli Style Sliced Monterey Jack Cheese

6 slices SARGENTO® Deli Style Sliced Medium Cheddar Cheese

Paprika (optional)

1. Melt butter in medium saucepan over medium heat. Stir in flour until smooth; cook 1 minute, stirring constantly. Stir in milk, salt and cayenne pepper. Heat to a boil; reduce heat. Simmer 1 minute or until thickened, stirring frequently. Stir in pasta.

2. Spoon half of pasta mixture into 8×8-inch square pan; top with Monterey Jack cheese. Repeat with remaining pasta and Cheddar cheese. Sprinkle with paprika, if desired. Bake in preheated 375°F oven 25 minutes or until bubbly.

Makes 6 servings

Cookies & Bars

Chippy Chewy Bars

½ cup (1 stick) butter or margarine

1½ cups graham cracker crumbs

1⅔ cups (10-ounce package) REESE'S® Peanut Butter Chips

1½ cups MOUNDS® Sweetened Coconut Flakes

1 can (14 ounces) sweetened condensed milk (not evaporated milk)

½ cup HERSHEY'S® SPECIAL DARK® Chocolate Chips, HERSHEY'S® Semi-Sweet Chocolate Chips or HERSHEY'S® Mini Chips Semi-Sweet Chocolate

¾ teaspoon shortening (do *not* use butter, margarine, spread or oil)

1. Heat oven to 350°F. Place butter in 13×9×2-inch baking pan. Heat in oven until melted; remove pan from oven. Sprinkle graham cracker crumbs evenly over butter; press down with fork.

2. Sprinkle peanut butter chips over crumbs; sprinkle coconut over chips. Drizzle sweetened condensed milk evenly over top.

3. Bake 20 minutes or until lightly browned.

4. Place chocolate chips and shortening in small microwave-safe bowl. Microwave at MEDIUM (50%) 30 seconds; stir. If necessary, microwave at MEDIUM an additional 10 seconds at a time, stirring after each heating, just until chips are melted when stirred. Drizzle evenly over top of baked mixture. Cool completely. Cut into bars.

Makes 24 bars

Best-Ever Peanut Butter-Oatmeal Cookies

2 cups quick-cooking oats

2 cups all-purpose flour

1 teaspoon baking powder

1 teaspoon baking soda

¼ teaspoon salt

1 cup butter

1 cup SKIPPY® Creamy Peanut Butter

1 cup granulated sugar

1 cup firmly packed brown sugar

2 eggs

2 teaspoons vanilla extract

1 (12 ounce) bag semisweet chocolate chips, if desired

Prep Time: 20 minutes
Bake Time: 13 minutes

1. Heat oven to 350°F.

2. In small bowl, combine oats, flour, baking powder, baking soda and salt; mix well.

3. In large bowl, beat together butter and peanut butter with electric mixer on medium speed until smooth. Beat in granulated and brown sugars, then eggs and vanilla until blended. Beat in flour mixture just until blended; stir in chocolate chips.

4. On ungreased baking sheets, drop dough by rounded tablespoonfuls 2 inches apart. Bake 13 minutes or until golden. Transfer cookies to wire rack to cool completely.

Makes 6 dozen cookies

MINI KISSES® Blondies

½ cup (1 stick) butter or margarine, softened

1⅓ cups packed light brown sugar

2 eggs

2 teaspoons vanilla extract

¼ teaspoon salt

2 cups all-purpose flour

1½ teaspoons baking powder

1¾ cups (10-ounce package) HERSHEY'S® MINI KISSES®BRAND Milk Chocolates

½ cup chopped nuts

1. Heat oven to 350°F. Lightly grease 13×9×2-inch baking pan.

2. Beat butter and brown sugar in large bowl until fluffy. Add eggs, vanilla and salt; beat until blended. Add flour and baking powder; beat just until blended. Stir in chocolate pieces. Spread batter in prepared pan. Sprinkle nuts over top.

3. Bake 28 to 30 minutes or until set and golden brown. Cool completely in pan on wire rack. Cut into bars.

Makes 24 bars

Red Velvet Cream Cheese Squares

- **1 package (16.25 ounces) white cake mix**
- **⅓ cup HERSHEY'S® Cocoa**
- **¾ cup sugar, divided**
- **½ cup (1 stick) butter or margarine, melted**
- **2 tablespoons (1-ounce bottle) red food color, divided**
- **1 tablespoon water**
- **3 eggs**
- **1 cup HERSHEY'S® SPECIAL DARK® Chocolate Chips or HERSHEY'S Semi-Sweet Chocolate Chips**
- **1 package (8 ounces) cream cheese, softened**
- **1 teaspoon vanilla extract**
- **1 container (8 ounces) dairy sour cream**
- **1 tablespoon milk**

1. Heat oven to 350°F. Line 13×9×2-inch baking pan with foil, extending foil beyond pan sides. Lightly grease foil.

2. Stir together cake mix, cocoa and ¼ cup sugar; set aside ½ cup cake mixture. Mix remaining cake mixture with melted butter, 1 tablespoon red food color, water and 1 egg until dough forms. Stir in chocolate chips. Press dough evenly on bottom of prepared pan.

3. Beat together cream cheese, remaining ½ cup sugar and vanilla until well blended. Beat in sour cream and remaining 2 eggs. Set aside ½ cup cream cheese mixture; pour remaining mixture in crust, spreading evenly.

4. Beat reserved cake mixture, reserved cream cheese mixture, remaining 1 tablespoon red food color and milk until well blended. Drop by tablespoons onto vanilla batter in pan. Swirl with knife for marbled effect.

5. Bake 30 to 35 minutes or until center is set. Cool completely in pan on wire rack. Cover; refrigerate until chilled. Cut into squares. Refrigerate leftovers.

Makes 24 squares

Cookie Pizza

1 package (16 to 18 ounces) refrigerated sugar cookie dough

12 assorted HERSHEY'S® MINIATURES® Chocolate Bars, unwrapped

¼ cup HERSHEY'S® SPECIAL DARK® Chocolate Chips, HERSHEY'S Semi-Sweet Chocolate Chips or HERSHEY'S® Milk Chocolate Chips

¼ cup REESE'S® Peanut Butter Chips

¼ cup HERSHEY'S Premier White Chips

1 bag (10½ ounces) miniature marshmallows

¼ cup HERSHEY'S® MILK DUDS® Candy made with chocolate and caramels

1. Heat oven to 350°F. Press cookie dough evenly into 11-inch circle on ungreased cookie sheet. Bake 15 to 17 minutes or until lightly browned. Meanwhile, break or cut chocolate bars into about ¼-inch pieces.

2. Remove cookie from oven. Evenly sprinkle surface with chocolate chips, peanut butter chips, white chips and chocolate bar pieces. Cover "toppings" with marshmallows. Sprinkle surface with chocolate-covered caramel candies. Return to oven; bake additional 5 minutes or until marshmallows are puffed and lightly browned. Cool. Cut into triangles.

Makes about 12 slices

Double Peanut Butter and Milk Chocolate Chip Cookies

½ cup (1 stick) butter or margarine, softened

¾ cup sugar

⅓ cup REESE'S® Creamy Peanut Butter

1 egg

½ teaspoon vanilla extract

1¼ cups all-purpose flour

½ teaspoon baking soda

¼ teaspoon salt

1 cup HERSHEY'S® Milk Chocolate Chips

1 cup REESE'S® Peanut Butter Chips

1. Heat oven to 350°F.

2. Beat butter, sugar and peanut butter in medium bowl until creamy. Add egg and vanilla; beat well. Stir together flour, baking soda and salt; add to butter mixture, blending well. Stir in milk chocolate chips and peanut butter chips. Drop by rounded teaspoons onto ungreased cookie sheets.

3. Bake 12 to 14 minutes or until light golden brown around edges. Cool 1 minute on cookie sheets. Remove to wire racks; cool completely.

Makes about 3 dozen cookies

Easy No-Bake Creamy Chocolate Mint Bars

2 cups (12-ounce package) NESTLÉ® TOLL HOUSE® Semi-Sweet Chocolate Morsels, *divided*

1 cup (2 sticks) butter, softened, *divided*

1¾ cups (about 30 cookies) finely crushed chocolate wafer cookies

2 tablespoons milk

1¼ teaspoons peppermint extract, *divided*

½ teaspoon vanilla extract

2½ cups powdered sugar

2 to 4 drops green food coloring

Prep Time: 20 minutes
Cooking Time: 5 minutes
Cooling Time: 2 hours 10 minutes

GREASE 9-inch-square baking pan.

MICROWAVE *⅓ cup* morsels and *⅓ cup* butter in small, uncovered, microwave-safe bowl on MEDIUM-HIGH (70%) power for 30 seconds; STIR. If necessary, microwave at additional 10- to 15-second intervals, stirring just until morsels are melted. Stir crushed cookies into melted morsel mixture. Press onto bottom of prepared pan. Refrigerate for 10 minutes or until firm.

MEANWHILE, BEAT *⅓ cup* butter, milk, *½ teaspoon* peppermint extract and vanilla extract in medium mixer bowl until smooth. Gradually beat in powdered sugar until smooth and creamy. Add food coloring, 1 drop at a time, until desired color is reached. Spread powdered sugar mixture evenly over cookie crumb layer.

MICROWAVE *remaining 1⅔ cups* morsels, *⅓ cup* butter and *¾ teaspoon* peppermint extract in small, uncovered, microwave-safe bowl on MEDIUM-HIGH (70%) power for 30 seconds; STIR. If necessary, microwave at additional 10- to 15-second intervals, stirring just until morsels are melted. Let stand for 10 minutes. Spread chocolate layer evenly over powdered sugar mixture. Refrigerate for at least 2 hours. For easier cutting, allow bars to sit at room temperature for 10 minutes.

Makes 25 servings

Original NESTLÉ® TOLL HOUSE® Chocolate Chip Cookies

- 2¼ **cups all-purpose flour**
- 1 **teaspoon baking soda**
- 1 **teaspoon salt**
- 1 **cup (2 sticks) butter, softened**
- ¾ **cup granulated sugar**
- ¾ **cup packed brown sugar**
- 1 **teaspoon vanilla extract**
- 2 **large eggs**
- 2 **cups (12-ounce package) NESTLÉ® TOLL HOUSE® Semi-Sweet Chocolate Morsels**
- 1 **cup chopped nuts**

Prep Time: 15 minutes
Baking Time: 9 minutes
Cooling Time: 15 minutes

PREHEAT oven to 375°F.

COMBINE flour, baking soda and salt in small bowl. Beat butter, granulated sugar, brown sugar and vanilla extract in large mixer bowl until creamy. Add eggs, one at a time, beating well after each addition. Gradually beat in flour mixture. Stir in morsels and nuts. Drop by rounded tablespoonful onto ungreased baking sheets.

BAKE for 9 to 11 minutes or until golden brown. Cool on baking sheets for 2 minutes; remove to wire racks to cool completely.

Makes about 5 dozen cookies

Pan Cookie Variation: GREASE 15×10-inch jelly-roll pan. Prepare dough as above. Spread in prepared pan. Bake for 20 to 25 minutes or until golden brown. Cool in pan on wire rack. Makes 4 dozen bars.

Double Chocolate KISSES® Cookies

- ½ cup (1 stick) butter or margarine, softened
- 1 cup sugar
- 1 egg
- 1½ teaspoons vanilla extract
- 1½ cups all-purpose flour
- ⅓ cup HERSHEY'S® Cocoa
- ½ teaspoon baking soda
- ¼ teaspoon salt
- ¼ cup milk
- 36 HERSHEY'S® KISSES®BRAND Milk Chocolates or HERSHEY'S® HUGS®BRAND Candies
- 1 can (16 ounces) vanilla ready-to-spread frosting

1. Beat butter, sugar, egg and vanilla in large bowl until well blended. Add flour, cocoa, baking soda and salt alternately with milk, beating until well blended. Cover; refrigerate dough about 1 hour or until firm enough to handle. Shape dough into 1-inch balls; place on ungreased cookie sheet.

2. Heat oven to 375°F. Remove wrappers from chocolate pieces.

3. Bake 8 to 10 minutes or until set. Cool 1 minute; remove from cookie sheet to wire rack. Cool completely. Spread frosting onto cookies, leaving about ½ inch around outer edge unfrosted; place chocolate piece in center of each cookie.

Makes about 3 dozen cookies

Oatmeal Scotchies

1 cup (2 sticks) margarine
   or butter, softened

¾ cup granulated sugar

¾ cup firmly packed brown
   sugar

2 eggs

1 teaspoon vanilla

1¼ cups all-purpose flour

1 teaspoon baking soda

½ teaspoon salt (optional)

3 cups QUAKER® Oats
   (quick or old fashioned,
   uncooked)

2 cups (12 ounces)
   butterscotch pieces

1. Heat oven to 375°F. Beat margarine and sugars in large bowl until creamy. Add eggs and vanilla; beat well. Combine flour, baking soda and salt, if desired, in small bowl; mix well. Add to creamed mixture; mix well. Add oats and butterscotch morsels; mix well.

2. Drop dough by level tablespoons onto ungreased cookie sheets.

3. Bake 7 to 8 minutes for chewy cookies or 9 to 10 minutes for crisp cookies. Cool 2 minutes on cookie sheets. Transfer to wire rack; cool completely. Store tightly covered.

Makes 48 cookies

Best Fudgey Pecan Brownies

½ cup (1 stick) butter or margarine, melted

1 cup sugar

1 teaspoon vanilla extract

2 eggs

½ cup all-purpose flour

⅓ cup HERSHEY'S® Cocoa

¼ teaspoon baking powder

¼ teaspoon salt

½ cup coarsely chopped pecans

CHOCOLATE PECAN FROSTING (recipe follows)

Pecan halves

1. Heat oven to 350°F. Lightly grease 8- or 9-inch square baking pan.

2. Beat butter, sugar and vanilla with spoon in large bowl. Add eggs; beat well. Stir together flour, cocoa, baking powder and salt; gradually add to egg mixture, beating until well blended. Stir in chopped pecans. Spread in prepared pan.

3. Bake 20 to 25 minutes or until brownies begin to pull away from sides of pan. Meanwhile, prepare CHOCOLATE PECAN FROSTING. Spread warm frosting over warm brownies. Garnish with pecan halves. Cool completely; cut into squares.

Makes about 16 brownies

Chocolate Pecan Frosting

1⅓ cups powdered sugar

2 tablespoons HERSHEY'S® Cocoa

3 tablespoons butter or margarine

2 tablespoons milk

¼ teaspoon vanilla extract

¼ cup chopped pecans

1. Stir together powdered sugar and cocoa in medium bowl.

2. Heat butter and milk in small saucepan over low heat until butter is melted. Gradually beat into cocoa mixture, beating until smooth. Stir in vanilla and pecans.

Makes about 1 cup frosting

Peanut Butter Blossoms

48 **HERSHEY'S® KISSES®**BRAND **Milk Chocolates**

¾ **cup REESE'S® Creamy Peanut Butter**

½ **cup shortening**

⅓ **cup granulated sugar**

⅓ **cup packed light brown sugar**

1 **egg**

2 **tablespoons milk**

1 **teaspoon vanilla extract**

1½ **cups all-purpose flour**

1 **teaspoon baking soda**

½ **teaspoon salt**

Additional granulated sugar

1. Heat oven to 375°F. Remove wrappers from chocolates.

2. Beat peanut butter and shortening with electric mixer on medium speed in large bowl until well blended. Add ⅓ cup granulated sugar and brown sugar; beat until fluffy. Add egg, milk and vanilla; beat well. Stir together flour, baking soda and salt; gradually beat into peanut butter mixture.

3. Shape dough into 1-inch balls. Roll in additional granulated sugar; place on ungreased cookie sheet.

4. Bake 8 to 10 minutes or until lightly browned. Immediately press a chocolate into center of each cookie; cookies will crack around edges. Remove to wire racks and cool completely.

Makes about 4 dozen cookies

Sweet & Salty
NESTLÉ® TOLL HOUSE® Cookies

2¼ cups all-purpose flour

1 teaspoon baking soda

1 teaspoon salt (optional)

1 cup (2 sticks) butter, softened

¾ cup granulated sugar

¾ cup packed brown sugar

1 teaspoon vanilla extract

2 large eggs

2 cups (12-ounce package) NESTLÉ® TOLL HOUSE® Semi-Sweet Chocolate Morsels

2 cups coarsely broken rippled potato chips

1 cup small pretzel twists, broken into ½-inch pieces

½ cup unsalted peanuts (optional)

Prep Time: 15 minutes
Baking Time: 9 minutes

PREHEAT oven to 375°F.

COMBINE flour, baking soda and salt in small bowl. Beat butter, granulated sugar, brown sugar and vanilla extract in large mixer bowl until creamy. Add eggs, one at a time, beating well after each addition. Gradually beat in flour mixture. Stir in morsels, potato chips, pretzel pieces and peanuts. Drop by rounded tablespoonful onto ungreased baking sheets.

BAKE for 9 to 11 minutes or until golden brown. Cool on baking sheets for 2 minutes; remove to wire racks to cool completely.

Makes 5 dozen cookies

Famous Oatmeal Cookies

¾ **cup firmly packed brown sugar**

¾ **cup trans-fat-free vegetable shortening**

½ **cup granulated sugar**

1 **egg**

¼ **cup water**

1 **teaspoon vanilla**

3 **cups QUAKER® Oats (quick or old fashioned, uncooked)**

1 **cup all-purpose flour**

1 **teaspoon salt (optional)**

½ **teaspoon baking soda**

1. Heat oven to 375°F. Beat brown sugar, shortening and granulated sugar in large bowl with electric mixer on medium speed until creamy. Add egg, water and vanilla; beat well. Add combined oats, flour, salt, if desired, and baking soda; mix well.

2. Drop dough by rounded teaspoonfuls onto ungreased cookie sheets.

3. Bake 9 to 11 minutes or until edges are golden brown. Remove to wire racks. Cool completely. Store tightly covered.

Makes about 60 cookies

Variations: Add 1 cup of any one or a combination of any of the following ingredients to basic cookie dough: raisins, chopped nuts, chocolate chips or shredded coconut.

Large Cookies: Drop dough by rounded tablespoonfuls onto ungreased cookie sheets. Bake 15 to 17 minutes. Makes about 30 cookies.

Bar Cookies: Press dough onto bottom of ungreased 13×9-inch baking pan. Bake 30 to 35 minutes or until light golden brown. Cool completely in pan on wire rack. Cut into bars. Store tightly covered. Makes 24 bars.

High-Altitude Adjustment: Increase flour to 1¼ cups and bake as directed.

Lemon Bars

CRUST

- **2 cups all-purpose flour**
- **½ cup powdered sugar**
- **1 cup (2 sticks) butter or margarine, softened**

FILLING

- **1 can (14 ounces) NESTLÉ® CARNATION® Sweetened Condensed Milk**
- **4 large eggs**
- **⅔ cup lemon juice**
- **1 tablespoon all-purpose flour**
- **1 teaspoon baking powder**
- **¼ teaspoon salt**
- **4 drops yellow food coloring (optional)**
- **1 tablespoon grated lemon peel**
- **Sifted powdered sugar (optional)**

Prep Time: 30 minutes
Baking Time: 40 minutes
Cooling Time: 2 hours refrigerating

PREHEAT oven to 350°F.

For Crust

COMBINE flour and powdered sugar in medium bowl. Cut in butter with pastry blender or two knives until mixture is crumbly. Press lightly onto bottom and halfway up sides of ungreased 13×9-inch baking pan.

BAKE for 20 minutes.

For Filling

BEAT sweetened condensed milk and eggs in large mixer bowl until fluffy. Beat in lemon juice, flour, baking powder, salt and food coloring just until blended. Fold in lemon peel; pour over crust.

BAKE for 20 to 25 minutes or until filling is set and crust is golden brown. Cool in pan on wire rack. Refrigerate for about 2 hours. Cut into bars; sprinkle with powdered sugar.

Makes 4 dozen bars

Peanut Butter Chocolate Bars

- **1 cup EQUAL® SPOONFUL***
- **½ cup stick butter or margarine, softened**
- **⅓ cup firmly packed brown sugar**
- **½ cup 2% milk**
- **½ cup creamy peanut butter**
- **1 egg**
- **1 teaspoon vanilla**
- **1 cup all-purpose flour**
- **¾ cup quick oats, uncooked**
- **½ teaspoon baking soda**
- **¼ teaspoon salt**
- **¾ cup mini semi-sweet chocolate chips**

*You may substitute 24 packets EQUAL® sweetener.

• Beat Equal®, butter and brown sugar until well combined. Stir in milk, peanut butter, egg and vanilla until blended. Gradually mix in combined flour, oats, baking soda and salt until blended. Stir in chocolate chips.

• Spread mixture evenly into 13×9-inch baking pan generously coated with nonstick cooking spray. Bake in preheated 350°F oven 20 to 22 minutes. Cool completely in pan on wire rack. Cut into bars; store in airtight container at room temperature.

Makes 48 bars

Milk Chocolate Florentine Cookies

⅔ cup butter

2 cups quick oats

1 cup granulated sugar

⅔ cup all-purpose flour

¼ cup light or dark corn syrup

¼ cup milk

1 teaspoon vanilla extract

¼ teaspoon salt

1¾ cups (11.5-ounce package) NESTLÉ® TOLL HOUSE® Milk Chocolate Morsels

Prep Time: 40 minutes
Cooking Time: 10 minutes

PREHEAT oven to 375°F. Line baking sheets with foil.

MELT butter in medium saucepan; remove from heat. Stir in oats, sugar, flour, corn syrup, milk, vanilla extract and salt; mix well. Drop by level teaspoonful, about 3 inches apart, onto prepared baking sheets. Spread thinly with rubber spatula.

BAKE for 6 to 8 minutes or until golden brown. Cool completely on baking sheets on wire racks. Peel foil from cookies.

MICROWAVE morsels in medium, uncovered, microwave-safe bowl on MEDIUM-HIGH (70%) power for 1 minute; STIR. Morsels may retain some of their original shape. If necessary, microwave at additional 10- to 15-second intervals, stirring just until morsels are melted. Spread thin layer of melted chocolate onto flat side of *half* the cookies. Top with *remaining* cookies.

Makes about 3½ dozen sandwich cookies

Variation: Pan Cookie Variation: Grease 15×10-inch jelly-roll pan. Prepare dough as above. Spread in prepared pan. Bake for 20 to 25 minutes or until golden brown. Cool in pan on wire rack.

Makes 4 dozen bars

Vanishing Oatmeal Raisin Cookies

½ cup (1 stick) plus
    6 tablespoons butter,
    softened

¾ cup firmly packed brown
    sugar

½ cup granulated sugar

2 eggs

1 teaspoon vanilla

1½ cups all-purpose flour

1 teaspoon baking soda

1 teaspoon ground cinnamon

½ teaspoon salt (optional)

3 cups QUAKER® Oats
    (quick or old fashioned,
    uncooked)

1 cup raisins

1. Heat oven to 350°F. Beat butter and sugars in large bowl with electric mixer on medium speed until creamy. Add eggs and vanilla; beat well. Add combined flour, baking soda, cinnamon and salt, if desired; mix well. Add oats and raisins; mix well.

2. Drop dough by rounded tablespoonfuls onto ungreased cookie sheets.

3. Bake 8 to 10 minutes or until light golden brown. Cool 1 minute on cookie sheets; remove to wire racks. Cool completely. Store tightly covered.

Makes 48 cookies

Variations: Stir in 1 cup chopped nuts. Substitute 1 cup semisweet chocolate chips or candy-coated chocolate pieces for raisins; omit cinnamon. Substitute 1 cup diced dried mixed fruit.

Bar Cookies: Press dough onto bottom of ungreased 13×9-inch baking pan. Bake 30 to 35 minutes or until light golden brown. Cool completely in pan on wire rack. Cut into bars. Store tightly covered. Makes 24 bars.

High-Altitude Adjustment: Increase flour to 1¾ cups and bake as directed.

Chocolate Macaroon Bars

1¼ cups graham cracker crumbs

⅓ cup sugar

¼ cup HERSHEY'S® Cocoa

⅓ cup butter or margarine, melted

1 can (14 ounces) sweetened condensed milk (not evaporated milk)

2⅔ cups MOUNDS® Sweetened Coconut Flakes

2 cups fresh white bread crumbs (about 5 slices)

2 eggs

2 teaspoons vanilla extract

1 cup HERSHEY'S® Mini Chips Semi-Sweet Chocolate

1. Heat oven to 350°F.

2. Stir together graham cracker crumbs, sugar, cocoa and butter in large bowl; press firmly onto bottom of ungreased 13×9×2-inch baking pan.

3. Bake 10 minutes. Meanwhile, combine sweetened condensed milk, coconut, bread crumbs, eggs, vanilla and small chocolate chips in large bowl; stir until blended. Spoon over prepared crust, spreading evenly.

4. Bake 30 minutes or until lightly browned. Cool completely in pan on wire rack. Cut into bars. Store covered in refrigerator.

Makes about 24 bars

Ultimate Chocolate Brownies

¾ cup HERSHEY'S® Cocoa

½ teaspoon baking soda

⅔ cup butter or margarine, melted and divided

½ cup boiling water

2 cups sugar

2 eggs

1⅓ cups all-purpose flour

1 teaspoon vanilla extract

¼ teaspoon salt

1 cup HERSHEY'S® SPECIAL DARK® Chocolate Chips or HERSHEY'S® Semi-Sweet Chocolate Chips

ONE-BOWL BUTTERCREAM FROSTING (recipe follows)

1. Heat oven to 350°F. Grease 13×9×2-inch baking pan or two 8-inch square baking pans.

2. Stir together cocoa and baking soda in large bowl; stir in ⅓ cup melted butter. Add boiling water; stir until mixture thickens. Stir in sugar, eggs and remaining ⅓ cup butter; stir until smooth. Add flour, vanilla and salt; blend completely. Stir in chocolate chips. Pour into prepared pan(s).

3. Bake 35 to 40 minutes for rectangular pan, 30 to 35 minutes for square pans or until brownies begin to pull away from sides of pan. Cool completely in pan on wire rack. Meanwhile, prepare ONE-BOWL BUTTERCREAM FROSTING. Frost brownies; cut into squares.

Makes about 36 brownies

One-Bowl Buttercream Frosting

6 tablespoons butter or margarine, softened

2⅔ cups powdered sugar

½ cup HERSHEY'S® Cocoa

⅓ cup milk

1 teaspoon vanilla extract

Beat butter in medium bowl. Add powdered sugar and cocoa alternately with milk, beating to spreading consistency (additional milk may be needed). Stir in vanilla.

Makes about 2 cups frosting

QUAKER's Best Oatmeal Cookies

1¼ cups (2½ sticks) margarine
     or butter, softened

¾ cup packed brown sugar

½ cup granulated sugar

1 egg

1 teaspoon vanilla

1½ cups all-purpose flour

1 teaspoon baking soda

1 teaspoon ground cinnamon

½ teaspoon salt (optional)

¼ teaspoon ground nutmeg

3 cups QUAKER® Oats
     (quick or old fashioned,
     uncooked)

1. Heat oven to 375°F. Beat margarine and sugars in large bowl until creamy. Add egg and vanilla; beat well. Combine flour, baking soda, cinnamon, salt, if desired, and nutmeg in medium bowl; mix well. Add to creamed mixture; mix well. Add oats; mix well.

2. Drop dough by rounded tablespoonfuls onto ungreased cookie sheets.

3. Bake 8 to 9 minutes for chewy cookies or 10 to 11 minutes for crisp cookies. Cool 1 minute on cookie sheets. Transfer to wire rack; cool completely. Store tightly covered.

Makes 36 cookies

Bar Cookies: Press dough onto bottom of ungreased 13×9-inch baking pan. Bake 25 to 30 minutes or until lightly golden brown. Cool completely in pan on wire rack. Cut into bars. Store tightly covered. Makes 24 bars.

Variations: Omit spices; stir in 1 cup chocolate chips, butterscotch-flavored chips or peanut butter-flavored chips. Stir in 1 cup raisins or chopped nuts.

Rich Cocoa Crinkle Cookies

- 2 cups granulated sugar
- ¾ cup vegetable oil
- 1 cup HERSHEY'S® Cocoa
- 4 eggs
- 2 teaspoons vanilla extract
- 2⅓ cups all-purpose flour
- 2 teaspoons baking powder
- ½ teaspoon salt
  Powdered sugar

1. Combine granulated sugar and oil in large bowl; add cocoa, beating until well blended. Beat in eggs and vanilla. Stir together flour, baking powder and salt. Gradually add to cocoa mixture, beating well.

2. Cover; refrigerate until dough is firm enough to handle, at least 6 hours.

3. Heat oven to 350°F. Lightly grease cookie sheet or line with parchment paper. Shape dough into 1-inch balls; roll in powdered sugar to coat. Place about 2 inches apart on prepared cookie sheet.

4. Bake 10 to 12 minutes or until almost no indentation remains when touched lightly and tops are crackled. Cool slightly. Remove from cookie sheet to wire rack. Cool completely.

Makes about 6 dozen cookies

Cakes & Tortes

Angel Lush with Pineapple

1 **can (20 ounces) DOLE®
Crushed Pineapple,
undrained**

1 **package (4-serving size)
instant vanilla pudding
and pie filling**

1 **cup thawed non-diary
whipped topping**

1 **prepared angel food cake**

Seasonal berries

Prep Time: 15 minutes
Chill Time: 1 hour

• Mix pineapple and dry pudding mix in medium bowl. Gently stir in whipped topping. Let stand 5 minutes.

• Cut cake horizontally into 3 layers. Place bottom cake layer, cut side up, on serving plate.

• Spread 1⅓ cups of the mixture onto cake layer; cover with middle cake layer. Spread 1 cup pudding onto middle cake layer; top with remaining cake layer. Spread with remaining pudding mixture. Refrigerate at least 1 hour or until ready to serve. Garnish with your favorite seasonal berries.

Makes 10 servings

Angel Lush Make It Your Way:
Angel Lush Shells: Prepare pudding mixture as above. Fill 12 dessert shells with filling; top with mixed berries.

Angel Lush Parfaits: Prepare pudding mixture as above. Layer cut-up angel food cake, filling and 2 cups mixed berries in 12 dessert glasses.

Tuxedo Torte

½ **cup (1 stick) butter or margarine, melted**

1¼ **cups granulated sugar**

1 **teaspoon vanilla extract**

2 **eggs**

⅔ **cup all-purpose flour**

½ **cup HERSHEY'S® Cocoa**

¼ **teaspoon baking powder**

¼ **teaspoon salt**

1 **package (8 ounces) cream cheese, softened**

1 **cup powdered sugar**

¾ **cup heavy cream, divided**

28 **HERSHEY'S® KISSES®BRAND Milk Chocolates***

Whipped topping or sweetened whipped cream (optional)

Additional HERSHEY'S® KISSES®BRAND Milk Chocolates (optional)

HERSHEY'S® HUGS®BRAND Candies (optional)

*¾ cup HERSHEY'S® MINI KISSES®BRAND Milk Chocolates may be substituted for HERSHEY'S® KISSES®BRAND Milk Chocolates.

1. Heat oven to 350°F. Line 9-inch round cake pan with foil, extending foil beyond sides. Grease foil.

2. Stir together melted butter, granulated sugar and vanilla in large bowl. Add eggs; beat well using spoon. Stir together flour, cocoa, baking powder and salt; gradually add to egg mixture, beating with spoon until well blended. Spread batter in prepared pan.

3. Bake 25 minutes or until cake is set. (Cake will be fudgey and will not test done.) Remove from oven; cool completely in pan on wire rack.

4. Beat cream cheese and powdered sugar in medium bowl until well blended. Beat ½ cup heavy cream until stiff; gradually fold into cream cheese mixture, blending well. Spread over brownie layer. Cover; refrigerate at least 1 hour.

5. Remove wrappers from 28 milk chocolates; place in medium microwave-safe bowl with remaining ¼ cup heavy cream. Microwave at MEDIUM (50%) 1 minute; stir. If necessary, microwave at MEDIUM an additional 10 seconds at a time, stirring after each heating, until chocolates are melted and mixture is smooth when stirred. Cool slightly; pour and spread over cream cheese mixture.

6. Cover; refrigerate about 2 hours or until chilled. Use foil to lift out of pan; remove foil. Cut into wedges; serve garnished with whipped topping, chocolates and chocolate candies, if desired. Cover; refrigerate leftover dessert.

Makes 12 servings

HERSHEY'S® Red Velvet Cake

½ cup (1 stick) butter or margarine, softened

1½ cups sugar

2 eggs

1 teaspoon vanilla extract

1 cup buttermilk or sour milk*

2 tablespoons (1-ounce bottle) red food color

2 cups all-purpose flour

⅓ cup HERSHEY'S® Cocoa

1 teaspoon salt

1½ teaspoons baking soda

1 tablespoon white vinegar

1 to 2 cans (16 ounces *each*) ready-to-spread vanilla frosting

HERSHEY'S® Mini Chips Semi-Sweet Chocolate, HERSHEY'S® Milk Chocolate Chips or red sugar sprinkles (optional)

*To sour milk: Use 1 tablespoon white vinegar plus milk to equal 1 cup.

1. Heat oven to 350°F. Grease and flour 13×9×2-inch baking pan.**

2. Beat butter and sugar in large bowl; add eggs and vanilla, beating well. Stir together buttermilk and food color. Stir together flour, cocoa and salt; add alternately to butter mixture with buttermilk mixture, mixing well. Stir in baking soda and vinegar. Pour into prepared pan.

3. Bake 30 to 35 minutes or until wooden pick inserted in center comes out clean. Cool completely in pan on wire rack. Frost; garnish with chocolate chips or red sugar sprinkles, if desired.

**This recipe can be made in two 9-inch cake pans. Bake at 350°F for 30 to 35 minutes or until wooden pick inserted in center comes out clean. Cool 10 minutes; remove from pans. Cool completely. Frost as directed.

Makes 12 servings

For Heart Shapes: Using open-topped heart-shaped cookie cutter (at least 1½ inches deep and 3 inches wide), cut cake into 12 hearts. Frost and decorate as directed.

HERSHEY'S® Red Velvet Cupcakes: Line about 28 muffin cups (2½ inches in diameter) with paper or foil bake cups. Prepare batter as above; fill each muffin cup about ½ full with batter. Bake at 350°F about 20 minutes or until wooden pick inserted in center comes out clean. Cool in pan on wire rack. Frost as directed. Makes about 28 cupcakes.

HERSHEY'S® HUGS® and KISSES® Candies Chocolate Cake

¾ cup (1½ sticks) butter or margarine, softened

1¾ cups sugar

2 eggs

1 teaspoon vanilla extract

2 cups all-purpose flour

¾ cup HERSHEY'S® Cocoa or HERSHEY'S® SPECIAL DARK® Cocoa

1¼ teaspoons baking soda

½ teaspoon salt

1⅓ cups water

COCOA FUDGE FROSTING (recipe follows)

HERSHEY'S® HUGS®BRAND Candies or HERSHEY'S® KISSES®BRAND Milk Chocolates

1. Heat oven to 350°F. Grease and flour 13×9×2-inch baking pan.

2. Beat butter and sugar in large bowl until fluffy. Add eggs and vanilla; beat 1 minute on medium speed of mixer. Stir together flour, cocoa, baking soda and salt; add alternately with water to butter mixture, beating until well blended. Pour batter into prepared pan.

3. Bake 40 to 45 minutes or until wooden pick inserted in center comes out clean. Cool 10 minutes; remove from pan to wire rack. Cool completely. Frost with COCOA FUDGE FROSTING. Remove wrappers from candies; garnish cake as desired with candies.

Makes 12 servings

Cocoa Fudge Frosting

½ cup (1 stick) butter or margarine

½ cup HERSHEY'S® Cocoa or HERSHEY'S® SPECIAL DARK® Cocoa

3⅔ cups (1 pound) powdered sugar

⅓ cup milk, heated

1 teaspoon vanilla extract

Melt butter in small saucepan over low heat; stir in cocoa. Cook, stirring constantly, until mixture thickens slightly. Remove from heat; pour into small mixer bowl. Add powdered sugar alternately with warm milk, beating to spreading consistency. Stir in vanilla. Spread frosting while warm.

Makes about 2½ cups frosting

No-Bake Cherry Chocolate Shortcake

1 **frozen loaf pound cake (10¾ ounces), thawed**

1 **can (21 ounces) cherry pie filling, chilled**

⅓ **cup HERSHEY'S® Cocoa or HERSHEY'S® SPECIAL DARK® Cocoa**

½ **cup powdered sugar**

1 **container (8 ounces) frozen non-dairy whipped topping, thawed (3 cups)**

1. Slice pound cake horizontally into three layers. Place bottom cake layer on serving plate; top with half of the pie filling, using mostly cherries. Repeat with middle cake layer and remaining pie filling; place rounded layer on top. Cover; refrigerate several hours.

2. Sift cocoa and powdered sugar onto whipped topping; stir until mixture is blended and smooth. Immediately spread over top and sides of cake, covering completely. Refrigerate leftover shortcake.

Makes about 6 servings

Mini Pumpkin Pecan Orange Soaked Cakes

½ **cup chopped pecans**

1 **package (18.25 ounces) spice cake mix**

1 **can (15 ounces) LIBBY'S® 100% Pure Pumpkin**

1 **cup vegetable oil**

4 **large eggs**

Orange Syrup (recipe follows)

Prep Time: 15 minutes
Cooking Time: 25 minutes
Cooling Time: 5 minutes

PREHEAT oven to 350°F. Grease and flour two 6-cake mini Bundt pans. Sprinkle nuts over bottom.

COMBINE cake mix, pumpkin, vegetable oil and eggs in large mixer bowl. Beat on low speed for 30 seconds or until blended. Beat for 4 minutes on medium speed. Spoon about ½ *cup* into each mold.

BAKE for 20 to 25 minutes or until wooden pick inserted in cakes comes out clean. Remove from oven. With back of spoon, carefully pat down dome of each cake to flatten. Let cool in pans for 5 minutes. Invert cakes onto cooling rack(s). Poke holes in cakes with wooden pick. Spoon a tablespoon of Orange Syrup over each cake. Allow syrup to soak in. Cool completely before serving or wrapping for gifts.

Makes 12 cakes

Orange Syrup: PLACE ¼ cup (½ stick) butter, ½ cup granulated sugar, 2 tablespoons water and 2 teaspoons grated orange peel in small saucepan. Bring to a boil. Remove from heat. Stir in 2 tablespoons orange juice.

Chocolate Rum Pecan Pound Cake

⅔ cup **HERSHEY'S® Cocoa, divided**

¼ cup **boiling water**

1¼ cups (2½ sticks) **butter or margarine, softened**

2⅔ cups **sugar**

1 teaspoon **vanilla extract**

5 **eggs**

2 cups **all-purpose flour**

1 teaspoon **salt**

½ teaspoon **baking powder**

¼ teaspoon **baking soda**

½ cup **buttermilk or sour milk***

¾ cup **finely chopped pecans**

¼ cup **light rum** *or*
  1½ **teaspoons rum extract plus ¼ cup water**

SATINY MINI CHIPS GLAZE (recipe follows)

*To sour milk: Use 1½ teaspoons white vinegar plus milk to equal ½ cup.

1. Heat oven to 325°F. Grease and flour 12-cup fluted tube pan.

2. Stir ⅓ cup cocoa and water in small bowl until smooth; set aside. Beat butter, sugar and vanilla in large bowl until fluffy. Add eggs, one at a time, beating well after each addition. Add reserved cocoa mixture; beat well. Stir together flour, remaining ⅓ cup cocoa, salt, baking powder and baking soda; add to butter mixture alternately with buttermilk, beating well after each addition. Stir in pecans and rum. Pour batter into prepared pan.

3. Bake 1 hour and 5 minutes or until wooden pick inserted in center comes out clean. Cool 10 minutes; remove from pan to wire rack. Cool completely. Prepare SATINY MINI CHIPS GLAZE; drizzle over cake.

Makes 12 servings

Satiny Mini Chips Glaze: Combine ¼ cup sugar and ¼ cup water in small saucepan. Cook over medium heat, stirring constantly, until sugar is dissolved and mixture begins to boil. Remove from heat; add 1 cup HERSHEY'S® Mini Chips Semi-Sweet Chocolate, stirring until melted. Continue stirring until glaze is of desired consistency. Makes about 1 cup glaze.

Triple Layer Cheesecake

CHOCOLATE CRUMB CRUST (recipe follows)

3 packages (8 ounces *each*) cream cheese, softened

¾ cup sugar

3 eggs

⅓ cup dairy sour cream

3 tablespoons all-purpose flour

1 teaspoon vanilla extract

¼ teaspoon salt

1 cup HERSHEY'S® Butterscotch Chips, melted*

1 cup HERSHEY'S® Premier White Chips, melted*

1 cup HERSHEY'S® SPECIAL DARK® Chocolate Chips or HERSHEY'S® Semi-Sweet Chocolate Chips, melted*

TRIPLE DRIZZLE (recipe follows, optional)

*To melt chips: Place chips in separate medium microwave-safe bowls. Microwave at MEDIUM (50%) 1 minute; stir. If necessary, microwave at MEDIUM an additional 15 seconds at a time, stirring after each heating, just until chips are melted when stirred.

1. Heat oven to 350°F. Prepare CHOCOLATE CRUMB CRUST.

2. Beat cream cheese and sugar in large bowl on medium speed of mixer until smooth. Add eggs, sour cream, flour, vanilla and salt; beat until blended. Stir 1⅓ cups batter into melted butterscotch chips until smooth; pour into prepared crust. Stir 1⅓ cups batter into melted white chips until smooth; pour over butterscotch layer. Stir remaining batter into melted chocolate chips until smooth; pour over white layer.

3. Bake 55 to 60 minutes or until almost set in center. Remove from oven to wire rack. With knife, immediately loosen cake from side of pan. Cool completely; remove side of pan. Prepare TRIPLE DRIZZLE, if desired; drizzle, one flavor at a time, over top of cheesecake. Refrigerate about 3 hours. Cover; refrigerate leftover cheesecake.

Makes 12 servings

Chocolate Crumb Crust: Heat oven to 350°F. Stir together 1½ cups vanilla wafer crumbs (about 45 wafers, crushed), ½ cup powdered sugar and ¼ cup HERSHEY'S® Cocoa; stir in ⅓ cup melted butter or margarine. Press mixture onto bottom and 1½ inches up side of 9-inch springform pan. Bake 8 minutes. Cool.

Triple Drizzle

1 tablespoon *each* HERSHEY'S® Butterscotch Chips, HERSHEY'S® Semi-Sweet Chocolate Chips* *and* HERSHEY'S® Premier White Chips

1½ teaspoons shortening (do *not* use butter, margarine, spread or oil), divided

*Substitute 1 tablespoon HERSHEY'S® SPECIAL DARK® Chocolate Chips for HERSHEY'S® Semi-Sweet Chocolate Chips, if desired.

Place 1 tablespoon HERSHEY'S® Butterscotch Chips and ½ teaspoon shortening in small microwave-safe bowl. Microwave at MEDIUM (50%) 30 to 45 seconds; stir. If necessary, microwave an additional 10 seconds at a time, stirring after each heating, just until chips are melted when stirred. Repeat procedure with 1 tablespoon HERSHEY'S® Semi-Sweet Chocolate Chips and HERSHEY'S® Premier White Chips.

Tomato Soup Spice Cake

2 cups all-purpose flour

1⅓ cups sugar

4 teaspoons baking powder

1½ teaspoons ground allspice

1 teaspoon baking soda

1 teaspoon ground cinnamon

½ teaspoon ground cloves

1 can (10¾ ounces) CAMPBELL'S® Condensed Tomato Soup

½ cup vegetable shortening

2 eggs

¼ cup water

Cream Cheese Frosting

Prep Time: 20 minutes
Bake Time: 40 minutes
Cool Time: 20 minutes

1. Heat the oven to 350°F. Grease **2** (8- or 9-inch) cake pans.

2. Stir the flour, sugar, baking powder, allspice, baking soda, cinnamon and cloves in a large bowl. Add the soup, shortening, eggs and water. Beat with an electric mixer on low speed just until blended. Increase the speed to high and beat for 4 minutes. Pour the batter into the pans.

3. Bake for 40 minutes or until a toothpick inserted in the centers come out clean. Let the cakes cool in the pans on wire racks for 20 minutes. Frost with the *Cream Cheese Frosting*.

Makes 12 servings

Cream Cheese Frosting: Beat **1 package** (8 ounces) cream cheese, softened, **2 tablespoons** milk and **1 teaspoon** vanilla extract in a medium bowl with an electric mixer on medium speed until the mixture is creamy. Slowly beat in **1 package** (16 ounces) confectioners' sugar until the frosting is desired consistency.

KITCHEN TIP

The cake can also be prepared in a 13×9-inch baking pan.

Mocha Brownie Nut Torte

1 **cup (2 sticks) butter**

1 **package (4 ounces) HERSHEY'S® Unsweetened Chocolate Baking Bar, broken into pieces**

4 **eggs**

1 **teaspoon vanilla extract**

2 **cups granulated sugar**

1 **cup all-purpose flour**

1 **cup finely chopped pecans**

1 **package (8 ounces) cream cheese, softened**

1 **cup powdered sugar**

½ **cup chilled whipping cream**

2 **to 3 teaspoons powdered instant coffee**

CHOCOLATE GLAZE (recipe follows)

1. Heat oven to 350°F. Line bottom and sides of 9-inch round cake pan with foil, extending foil beyond sides. Grease foil.

2. Place butter and chocolate in medium microwave-safe bowl. Microwave at MEDIUM (50%) 1 minute; stir. If necessary, microwave an additional 15 seconds at a time, stirring after each heating, until chocolate is melted when stirred. Cool 5 minutes.

3. Beat eggs and vanilla in large bowl until foamy. Gradually beat in granulated sugar. Blend in chocolate mixture; fold in flour and pecans. Spread mixture in prepared pan. Bake 40 to 45 minutes or until wooden pick inserted in center comes out clean. Cool completely in pan on wire rack.

4. Use foil to lift brownie from pan; remove foil. Place brownie layer on serving plate. Beat cream cheese and powdered sugar in medium bowl until well blended. Beat whipping cream and instant coffee until stiff; gradually fold into cream cheese mixture, blending well. Spread over brownie layer. Cover; refrigerate until serving time.

5. Just before serving, prepare CHOCOLATE GLAZE. Drizzle generous tablespoon glaze over top and down sides of each serving.

Makes 12 servings

Chocolate Glaze: Place 6 ounces (1½ 4-ounce packages) HERSHEY'S® Semi-Sweet Chocolate Baking Bar and ½ cup whipping cream in small microwave-safe bowl. Microwave at MEDIUM (50%) 30 to 45 seconds or until chocolate is melted and mixture is smooth when stirred. Cool slightly. Makes 1 cup glaze.

HERSHEY'S® Lavish Chocolate Cake

1¼ cups all-purpose flour

⅓ cup HERSHEY'S® Cocoa

1 teaspoon baking soda

   Dash salt

½ cup (1 stick) butter

1 cup sugar

1 cup milk

1 tablespoon white vinegar

½ teaspoon vanilla extract

   CHOCOLATE MOUSSE
   FILLING (recipe follows)

2 to 4 tablespoons
   seedless black raspberry
   preserves

   CHOCOLATE GANACHE
   (recipe follows)

   Sweetened whipped cream

   Fresh raspberries
   (optional)

   Additional HERSHEY'S®
   Cocoa (optional)

1. Heat oven to 350°F. Line bottoms of three 8-inch round baking pans with wax paper. Lightly grease sides of pans. Combine flour, cocoa, baking soda and salt; set aside.

2. Place butter in large microwave-safe bowl. Microwave at MEDIUM (50%) 1 minute or until melted; stir in sugar. Add milk, vinegar and vanilla; stir until blended. Add dry ingredients; whisk until well blended. Pour batter evenly into prepared pans.

3. Bake 15 minutes or until wooden pick inserted in center comes out clean. Cool 10 minutes. Remove from pans to wire racks; gently peel off wax paper. Cool completely.

4. Prepare CHOCOLATE MOUSSE FILLING. Place one cake layer on serving plate; spread 2 tablespoons preserves over top. Carefully spread half of filling over preserves to within 1 inch of edge. Refrigerate about 10 minutes. Place second layer on top; repeat procedure with remaining preserves and filling. Place remaining layer on top. Refrigerate while preparing CHOCOLATE GANACHE. Spread ganache over top and sides of cake.

5. Refrigerate at least 30 minutes. At serving time, raspberries, if desired; sift additional cocoa over top, if desired. Refrigerate leftover cake.

Makes 12 servings

Chocolate Ganache

1 cup (½ pint) whipping
   cream

1½ cups HERSHEY'S®
   SPECIAL DARK®
   Chocolate Chips or
   HERSHEY'S® Semi-Sweet
   Chocolate Chips

Heat whipping cream in small heavy saucepan over low heat until warm. Add chocolate chips; stir constantly, just until chips are melted and mixture is smooth. Do not let mixture come to a boil. Transfer mixture to medium bowl; refrigerate until of spreading consistency (about 1½ hours).

Makes about 1⅔ cups ganache

Chocolate Mousse Filling

1 teaspoon unflavored
  gelatin

1 tablespoon cold water

2 tablespoons boiling water

½ cup sugar

¼ cup HERSHEY'S® Cocoa

1 cup (½ pint) cold
  whipping cream

1 teaspoon vanilla extract

1. Sprinkle gelatin over cold water in medium bowl; let stand 1 minute to soften. Add boiling water; stir until gelatin is completely dissolved and mixture is clear. Cool slightly.

2. Stir together sugar and cocoa in small bowl; add whipping cream and vanilla. Beat at medium speed of mixer, scraping bottom of bowl occasionally, until stiff; pour in gelatin mixture. Beat until well blended. Refrigerate about 20 minutes.

Makes 2 cups filling

Super Moist Chocolate Mayo Cake

1 box (18 ounces) chocolate
   cake mix
1 cup HELLMANN'S® or BEST
   FOODS® Real Mayonnaise
1 cup water
3 eggs
1 teaspoon ground cinnamon
   (optional)

Prep Time: 5 minutes
Cooking Time: 30 minutes

1. Preheat oven to 350°F. Grease and lightly flour two 9-inch round cake pans*; set aside.

2. Beat cake mix, HELLMANN'S® or BEST FOODS® Real Mayonnaise, water, eggs and cinnamon 30 seconds in large bowl with electric mixer on low speed. Beat on medium speed, scraping sides occasionally, 2 minutes. Pour into prepared pans.

3. Bake 30 minutes or until toothpick inserted in center comes out clean. Cool on wire racks 10 minutes. Remove cakes from pans and cool completely. Fill and frost, if desired, or sprinkle with confectioners sugar.

*OR, prepare cake mix as above in 13×9-inch baking pan and bake 40 minutes or until toothpick inserted in center comes out clean.

Makes 12 servings

Variation: For **PECAN-COCONUT TOPPED CAKE**, combine 1 cup flaked coconut, ⅔ cup firmly packed brown sugar and ½ cup chopped pecans, then sprinkle over cake batter in 13×9-inch baking pan. Bake 1 hour or until toothpick inserted in center comes out clean.

Variation: For **DECADENT CHOCOLATE LAVA CAKE**, combine 2 packages (3.4 ounces each) instant pudding, 2 cups water, 2 cups milk and ⅓ cup sugar until blended, then pour over cake batter in 13×9-inch baking pan. Bake 1 hour or until toothpick inserted along edge comes out clean; serve warm.

Variation: For **YELLOW MAYONNAISE CAKE**, substitute 1 box (18 ounces) yellow cake mix for the chocolate cake mix.

Variation: For **BLACK FOREST CHOCOLATE CAKE**, do not flour baking pan. Evenly spread 2 cans (21 ounces each) cherry pie filling over bottom of 13×9-inch baking pan, top with prepared cake batter and bake 1 hour or until toothpick inserted in center comes out clean. Cool completely, then turn upside down onto serving platter.

Pineapple Upside-Down Minis

2 cans (20 ounces each) DOLE® Pineapple Slices

⅓ cup butter or margarine, melted

⅔ cup packed brown sugar

9 maraschino cherries, cut in half

1 package (18¼ ounces) yellow or pineapple-flavored cake mix

• Drain pineapple; reserve juice.

• Stir together melted butter and brown sugar. Evenly divide sugar mixture into 18 (⅔-cup*) muffin cups, sprayed with nonstick vegetable cooking spray. Lightly press well-drained pineapple slices into sugar mixture. Place cherries in center of pineapple, sliced sides up.

• Prepare cake mix according to package directions, replacing amount of water called for with reserved juice. Pour ⅓ cup batter into each muffin cup.

• Bake at 350°F., for 20 to 25 minutes or until toothpick inserted in center comes out clean.

• Cool 5 minutes. Loosen edges and invert onto cookie sheets.

*If muffin cup is smaller than ⅔ cup, it will not be large enough to hold pineapple and batter.

Makes 18 servings

BREYERS® Ice Cream Birthday Cake

1 box (18¼ ounces) devil's food cake mix

1 container (1½ quarts) your favorite BREYERS® All Natural Ice Cream

1 container (8 ounces) frozen whipped topping, thawed

1 jar (7½ ounces) marshmallow creme

Prep Time: 30 minutes
Cook Time: 25 minutes
Freeze Time: 8 hours

1. Preheat oven to 350°F. Prepare cake mix according to package directions, baking in two 8-inch baking pans. Cool on wire racks 15 minutes. Remove cakes from pans and cool completely. Trim tops of cakes to flatten. Wrap cakes in aluminum foil and freeze at least 2 hours.

2. Remove cakes from foil. Arrange 1 cake on serving platter. Scoop BREYERS® All Natural Ice Cream onto cake, smoothing to form an even layer. Top with second cake, pressing down slightly. Freeze 5 hours or overnight.

3. Beat whipped topping with marshmallow creme in large bowl with wire whisk until smooth. Frost cake with whipped topping mixture. Freeze 1 hour. Decorate as desired.

Makes 20 servings

HERSHEY'S® White and Dark Chocolate Fudge Torte

1 cup (2 sticks) butter or
   margarine, melted

1½ cups sugar

1 teaspoon vanilla extract

3 eggs, separated

⅔ cup HERSHEY'S® Cocoa

½ cup all-purpose flour

3 tablespoons water

2 cups (12-ounce package)
   HERSHEY'S® Premier
   White Chips, divided

⅛ teaspoon cream of tartar

SATINY GLAZE (recipe
   follows)

WHITE DECORATOR
   DRIZZLE (recipe follows)

1. Heat oven to 350°F. Line bottom of 9-inch springform pan with foil; grease foil and side of pan.

2. Combine butter, sugar and vanilla in large bowl; beat well. Add egg yolks, one at a time, beating well after each addition. Blend in cocoa, flour and water. Stir in 1⅔ cups white chips. Reserve remaining chips for drizzle. Beat egg whites with cream of tartar in small bowl until stiff peaks form; fold into chocolate mixture. Pour batter into prepared pan.

3. Bake 45 minutes or until top begins to crack slightly. (Cake will not test done in center.) Cool 1 hour. Cover; refrigerate until firm. Remove side of pan. Prepare SATINY GLAZE and WHITE DECORATOR DRIZZLE. Pour prepared glaze over torte; spread evenly over top and sides. Decorate top of torte with prepared drizzle* *or* wait to prepare drizzle and decorate individual slices before serving. Cover; refrigerate until serving time. Refrigerate leftover torte.

*To decorate, drizzle with spoon or place in pastry bag with writing tip.

Makes 10 to 12 servings

Satiny Glaze

1 cup HERSHEY'S® SPECIAL
   DARK® Chocolate Chips or
   HERSHEY'S® Semi-Sweet
   Chocolate Chips

¼ cup whipping cream

Place chocolate chips and whipping cream in small microwave-safe bowl. Microwave at MEDIUM (50%) 1 minute; stir. If necessary, microwave at MEDIUM an additional 15 seconds at a time, stirring after each heating, just until chips are melted when stirred. Cool until lukewarm and slightly thickened.

Makes about ¾ cup glaze

White Decorator Drizzle

⅓ **cup HERSHEY'S® Premier White Chips (reserved from torte)**

2 **teaspoons shortening (do *not* use butter, margarine, spread or oil)**

Place white chips and shortening in small microwave-safe bowl. Microwave at MEDIUM (50%) 20 to 30 seconds; stir. If necessary, microwave at MEDIUM an additional 10 seconds at a time, stirring after each heating, just until chips are melted when stirred.

HERSHEY'S® KISSES® Birthday Cake

2 cups sugar

1¾ cups all-purpose flour

¾ cup HERSHEY'S® Cocoa or HERSHEY'S® SPECIAL DARK® Cocoa

1½ teaspoons baking powder

1½ teaspoons baking soda

1 teaspoon salt

2 eggs

1 cup milk

½ cup vegetable oil

2 teaspoons vanilla extract

1 cup boiling water

VANILLA BUTTERCREAM FROSTING (recipe follows)

HERSHEY'S® KISSES®BRAND Milk Chocolates

1. Heat oven to 350°F. Grease and flour two (9-inch) round baking pans or one (13×9×2-inch) baking pan.

2. Stir together sugar, flour, cocoa, baking powder, baking soda and salt in large bowl. Add eggs, milk, oil and vanilla; beat with electric mixer on medium speed for 2 minutes. Stir in boiling water (batter will be thin). Pour batter into prepared pans.

3. Bake 30 to 35 minutes for round pans, 35 to 40 minutes for rectangular pan or until wooden pick inserted in center comes out clean. Cool 10 minutes; turn out onto wire racks. Cool completely.

4. Frost with VANILLA BUTTERCREAM FROSTING. Remove wrappers from chocolates. Garnish top and sides of cake with chocolates.

Makes 12 servings

Vanilla Buttercream Frosting

⅓ cup butter or margarine, softened

4 cups powdered sugar, divided

3 to 4 tablespoons milk

1½ teaspoons vanilla extract

Beat butter with electric mixer on medium speed in large bowl until creamy. With mixer running, gradually add about 2 cups powdered sugar, beating until well blended. Slowly beat in milk and vanilla. Gradually add remaining powdered sugar, beating until smooth. Add additional milk, if necessary, until frosting is desired consistency.

Makes about 2⅓ cups frosting

Old-Fashioned Chocolate Cake

¾ cup (1½ sticks) butter or margarine, softened

1⅔ cups sugar

3 eggs

1 teaspoon vanilla extract

2 cups all-purpose flour

⅔ cup HERSHEY'S® Cocoa

1¼ teaspoons baking soda

1 teaspoon salt

¼ teaspoon baking powder

1⅓ cups water

½ cup finely crushed hard peppermint candy (optional)

ONE-BOWL BUTTERCREAM FROSTING (recipe follows)

Additional crushed hard peppermint candy (optional)

1. Heat oven to 350°F. Grease and flour two 9-inch round baking pans or one 13×9×2-inch baking pan.

2. Combine butter, sugar, eggs and vanilla in large bowl; beat on high speed of mixer 3 minutes. Stir together flour, cocoa, baking soda, salt and baking powder; add alternately with water to butter mixture. Blend just until combined; add candy, if desired. Pour batter into prepared pans.

3. Bake 30 to 35 minutes or until wooden pick inserted in center comes out clean. Cool 10 minutes; remove from pans to wire racks. Cool completely.

4. Frost with ONE-BOWL BUTTERCREAM FROSTING. Just before serving, garnish with peppermint candy, if desired.

Makes 12 servings

One-Bowl Buttercream Frosting

6 tablespoons butter or margarine, softened

2⅔ cups powdered sugar

½ cup HERSHEY'S® Cocoa

⅓ cup milk

1 teaspoon vanilla extract

Beat butter in medium bowl. Add powdered sugar and cocoa alternately with milk, beating to spreading consistency (additional milk may be needed). Stir in vanilla.

Makes about 2 cups frosting

Zesty Lemon Pound Cake

1 cup (6 ounces) NESTLÉ® TOLL HOUSE® Premier White Morsels

2½ cups all-purpose flour

1 teaspoon baking powder

½ teaspoon salt

1 cup (2 sticks) butter, softened

1½ cups granulated sugar

2 teaspoons vanilla extract

3 large eggs

3 to 4 tablespoons freshly grated lemon peel (about 3 medium lemons)

1⅓ cups buttermilk

1 cup powdered sugar

3 tablespoons fresh lemon juice

Prep Time: 20 minutes
Cooking Time: 55 minutes

PREHEAT oven to 350°F. Grease and flour 12-cup Bundt pan.

MELT morsels in medium, uncovered, microwave-safe bowl on MEDIUM–HIGH (70%) power for 1 minute. STIR. Morsels may retain some of their original shape. If necessary, microwave at additional 10- to 15-second intervals, stirring just until morsels are melted. Cool slightly.

COMBINE flour, baking powder and salt in small bowl. Beat butter, granulated sugar and vanilla extract in large mixer bowl until creamy. Beat in eggs, one at a time, beating well after each addition. Beat in lemon peel and melted morsels. Gradually beat in flour mixture alternately with buttermilk. Pour into prepared Bundt pan.

BAKE for 50 to 55 minutes or until wooden pick inserted into cake comes out clean. Cool in pan on wire rack for 10 minutes. Combine powdered sugar and lemon juice in small bowl. Make holes in cake with wooden pick; pour *half* of lemon glaze over cake. Let stand for 5 minutes. Invert onto plate. Make holes in top of cake; pour *remaining* glaze over cake. Cool completely before serving.

Makes 12 to 16 servings

Berry-Berry Brownie Torte

½ **cup all-purpose flour**

¼ **teaspoon baking soda**

¼ **teaspoon salt**

1 **cup HERSHEY'S® SPECIAL DARK® Chocolate Chips or HERSHEY'S® Semi-Sweet Chocolate Chips**

½ **cup (1 stick) butter or margarine**

1¼ **cups sugar, divided**

2 **eggs**

1 **teaspoon vanilla extract**

⅓ **cup HERSHEY'S® SPECIAL DARK® Cocoa or HERSHEY'S® Cocoa**

½ **cup whipping cream**

¾ **cup fresh blackberries, rinsed and patted dry**

¾ **cup fresh raspberries, rinsed and patted dry**

1. Heat oven to 350°F. Line 9-inch round baking pan with wax paper, then grease. Stir together flour, baking soda and salt. Stir in chocolate chips.

2. Melt butter in medium saucepan over low heat. Remove from heat. Stir in 1 cup sugar, eggs and vanilla. Add cocoa, blending well. Stir in flour mixture. Spread mixture in prepared pan.

3. Bake 20 to 25 minutes or until wooden pick inserted into center comes out slightly sticky. Cool in pan on wire rack 15 minutes. Invert onto wire rack; remove wax paper. Turn right side up; cool completely.

4. Beat whipping cream and remaining ¼ cup sugar until sugar is dissolved and stiff peaks form. Spread over top of brownie. Top with berries. Refrigerate until serving time.

Makes 12 servings

Surprise Prize Cupcakes

1 package (18.25 ounces) plain chocolate cake mix

⅓ cup water

3 large eggs

⅓ cup vegetable oil

1 package (16.5 ounces) NESTLÉ® TOLL HOUSE® Refrigerated Chocolate Chip Cookie Bar Dough

1 container (16 ounces) prepared chocolate frosting

NESTLÉ® TOLL HOUSE® Semi-Sweet Chocolate Mini Morsels morsels

Prep Time: 15 minutes
Baking Time: 19 minutes
Cooling Time: 30 minutes

PREHEAT oven to 350°F. Paper-line 24 muffin cups.

BEAT cake mix, water, eggs and oil in large mixer bowl on low speed for 30 seconds. Beat on medium speed for 2 minutes or until smooth. Spoon about ¼ cup batter into each cup, filling about two-thirds full.

CUT cookie dough into 24 pieces; roll each into a ball. Place one ball of dough in each muffin cup, pressing it into the bottom.

BAKE for 19 to 22 minutes or until top springs back when gently touched. Let stand for 15 minutes. Remove to wire rack to cool completely. Spread with frosting and sprinkle with morsels.

Makes 2 dozen cupcakes

Holiday Chocolate Cake

2 **cups sugar**

1¾ **cups all-purpose flour**

¾ **cup HERSHEY'S® Cocoa**

2 **teaspoons baking soda**

1 **teaspoon baking powder**

1 **teaspoon salt**

1 **cup buttermilk or sour milk***

1 **cup strong black coffee or 2 teaspoons powdered instant coffee dissolved in 1 cup hot water**

½ **cup vegetable oil**

2 **eggs**

2 **teaspoons vanilla extract**

RICOTTA CHEESE FILLING (recipe follows)

CHOCOLATE WHIPPED CREAM (recipe follows)

VANILLA WHIPPED CREAM (recipe follows)

Candied red or green cherries (optional)

*To sour milk: Use 1 tablespoon white vinegar plus milk to equal 1 cup.

1. Heat oven to 350°F. Grease and flour two 9-inch round baking pans.

2. Stir together sugar, flour, cocoa, baking soda, baking powder and salt in large bowl. Add buttermilk, coffee, oil, eggs and vanilla; beat at medium speed of mixer 2 minutes (batter will be thin). Pour batter into prepared pans.

3. Bake 30 to 35 minutes or until wooden pick inserted into center of cakes come out clean. Cool 10 minutes; remove from pans to wire racks. Cool completely.

4. Slice cake layers in half horizontally. Place bottom slice on serving plate; top with ⅓ RICOTTA CHEESE FILLING. Alternate cake layers and filling, ending with cake on top. Frost cake with CHOCOLATE WHIPPED CREAM. Decorate with VANILLA WHIPPED CREAM and cherries, if desired. Cover; refrigerate leftover cake.

Makes 12 servings

Chocolate Whipped Cream: Stir together ⅓ cup powdered sugar and 2 tablespoons HERSHEY'S® Cocoa in small bowl. Add 1 cup (½ pint) cold whipping cream and 1 teaspoon vanilla extract; beat until stiff.

Vanilla Whipped Cream: Beat ½ cup cold whipping cream, 2 tablespoons powdered sugar and ½ teaspoon vanilla extract in small bowl until stiff.

Ricotta Cheese Filling

1¾ cups (15 ounces) ricotta cheese*

¼ cup sugar

3 tablespoons Grand Marnier (orange-flavored liqueur) or orange juice concentrate, undiluted

¼ cup candied red or green cherries, coarsely chopped

⅓ cup HERSHEY'S® Mini Chips Semi-Sweet Chocolate

*1 cup (½ pint) whipping cream can be substituted for ricotta cheese. Beat with sugar and liqueur until stiff.

Beat ricotta cheese, sugar and liqueur in large bowl until smooth. Fold in candied cherries and small chocolate chips.

Desserts & Beverages

HERSHEY'S® Cocoa Cream Pie

1 baked (9-inch) pie crust
  or graham cracker crumb
  crust, cooled

1¼ cups sugar

½ cup HERSHEY'S® Cocoa

⅓ cup cornstarch

¼ teaspoon salt

3 cups milk

3 tablespoons butter or
  margarine

1½ teaspoons vanilla extract

Sweetened whipped
  cream

1. Prepare crust; cool.

2. Stir together sugar, cocoa, cornstarch and salt in medium saucepan. Gradually add milk, stirring until smooth. Cook over medium heat, stirring constantly, until mixture comes to a boil; boil 1 minute.

3. Remove from heat; stir in butter and vanilla. Pour into prepared crust. Press plastic wrap directly onto surface. Cool to room temperature. Refrigerate 6 to 8 hours. Serve with sweetened whipped cream. Garnish as desired. Cover; refrigerate leftover pie.

Makes 8 servings

CARNATION® Key Lime Pie

1 *prepared* 9-inch (6 ounces) graham cracker crumb crust

1 can (14 ounces) NESTLÉ® CARNATION® Sweetened Condensed Milk

½ cup (about 3 medium limes) fresh lime juice

1 teaspoon grated lime peel

2 cups frozen whipped topping, thawed

Lime peel twists or lime slices (optional)

Prep Time: 5 minutes
Cooling Time: 2 hours refrigerating

BEAT sweetened condensed milk and lime juice in small mixer bowl until combined; stir in lime peel. Pour into crust; spread with whipped topping. Refrigerate for 2 hours or until set. Garnish with lime peel twists.

Makes 8 servings

TOLL HOUSE®
Chocolate Chip Cookie Milkshake

1 pint (2 cups) vanilla ice cream

2 cups (about 8) freshly baked and crumbled **NESTLÉ® TOLL HOUSE® Refrigerated Chocolate Chip Cookies**

1 cup milk *or* ⅔ cup (5-ounce can) **NESTLÉ® CARNATION® Evaporated Milk, chilled**

Prep Time: 5 minutes

PLACE ice cream, cookies and *1 cup* milk *or* ⅔ cup (5-ounce can) NESTLÉ® CARNATION® Evaporated Milk in blender; cover. Blend until smooth. If a smoother shake is desired, add some additional milk.

Makes 3 servings

Fresh Lemon Meringue Pie

1½ **cups sugar**

¼ **cup plus 2 tablespoons cornstarch**

½ **teaspoon salt**

½ **cup cold water**

½ **cup freshly squeezed SUNKIST® lemon juice**

3 **egg yolks, well beaten**

2 **tablespoons butter or margarine**

1½ **cups boiling water**

Grated peel of ½ SUNKIST® lemon

2 **to 3 drops yellow food coloring (optional)**

1 **(9-inch) baked pie crust**

Three-Egg Meringue (recipe follows)

In large saucepan, combine sugar, cornstarch and salt. Gradually blend in cold water and lemon juice. Stir in egg yolks. Add butter and boiling water. Bring to a boil over medium-high heat, stirring constantly. Reduce heat to medium and boil 1 minute. Remove from heat; stir in lemon peel and food coloring. Pour into baked pie crust. Top with Three-Egg Meringue, sealing well at edges. Bake at 350°F 12 to 15 minutes. Cool 2 hours before serving.

Makes 6 servings

Three-Egg Meringue

3 **egg whites**

¼ **teaspoon cream of tartar**

6 **tablespoons sugar**

In large bowl with electric mixer, beat egg whites with cream of tartar until foamy. Gradually add sugar and beat until stiff peaks form.

LIBBY'S® Famous Pumpkin Pie

¾ cup granulated sugar

 1 teaspoon ground cinnamon

 ½ teaspoon salt

 ½ teaspoon ground ginger

 ¼ teaspoon ground cloves

 2 large eggs

 1 can (15 ounces) LIBBY'S® 100% Pure Pumpkin

 1 can (12 fluid ounces) NESTLÉ® CARNATION® Evaporated Milk

 1 *unbaked* 9-inch (4-cup volume) deep-dish pie shell

    Whipped cream

Prep Time: 15 minutes
Baking Time: 55 minutes
Cooling Time: 2 hours

≡ TIP

You can substitute *1¾ teaspoons* pumpkin pie spice for the cinnamon, ginger and cloves; however, the flavor will be slightly different.

MIX sugar, cinnamon, salt, ginger and cloves in small bowl. Beat eggs in large bowl. Stir in pumpkin and sugar-spice mixture. Gradually stir in evaporated milk.

POUR into pie shell.

BAKE in preheated 425°F oven for 15 minutes. Reduce oven temperature to 350°F; bake for 40 to 50 minutes or until knife inserted near center comes out clean. Cool on wire rack for 2 hours. Serve immediately or refrigerate. Top with whipped cream before serving.

Makes 8 servings

Note: Do not freeze this pie because this will result in the crust separating from the filling.

For 2 shallow pies: Substitute two 9-inch (2-cup volume) pie shells. Bake in preheated 425°F oven for 15 minutes. Reduce temperature to 350°F; bake for 20 to 30 minutes or until pies test done.

Hot Mulled Cider

½ **gallon apple cider**

½ **cup packed brown sugar**

1½ **teaspoons balsamic or cider vinegar (optional)**

1 **teaspoon vanilla**

1 **cinnamon stick**

6 **whole cloves**

½ **cup applejack or bourbon (optional)**

Prep Time: 5 minutes
Cook Time: 5 to 6 hours (LOW)

Combine cider, brown sugar, vinegar, if desired, vanilla, cinnamon stick and cloves in **CROCK-POT**® slow cooker. Cover; cook on LOW 5 to 6 hours. Remove and discard cinnamon stick and cloves. Stir in applejack just before serving, if desired. Serve warm in mugs.

Makes 16 servings

Classic Boston Cream Pie

⅓ cup shortening

1 cup sugar

2 eggs

1 teaspoon vanilla extract

1¼ cups all-purpose flour

1½ teaspoons baking powder

¼ teaspoon salt

¾ cup milk

    RICH FILLING (recipe follows)

    DARK COCOA GLAZE (recipe follows)

1. Heat oven to 350°F. Grease and flour 9-inch round baking pan.

2. Beat shortening, sugar, eggs and vanilla in large bowl until fluffy. Stir together flour, baking powder and salt; add alternately with milk to shortening mixture, beating well after each addition. Pour batter into prepared pan.

3. Bake 30 to 35 minutes or until wooden pick inserted in center comes out clean. Cool 10 minutes; remove from pan to wire rack. Cool completely.

4. Prepare RICH FILLING. With long serrated knife, cut cake in half horizontally. Place one layer, cut side up, on serving plate; spread with prepared filling. Top with remaining layer, cut side down. Prepare DARK COCOA GLAZE; spread over cake, allowing glaze to run down sides. Refrigerate several hours or until cold. Garnish as desired. Refrigerate leftover dessert.

Makes 12 servings

Rich Filling

⅓ cup sugar

2 tablespoons cornstarch

1½ cups milk

2 egg yolks, slightly beaten

1 tablespoon butter or margarine

1 teaspoon vanilla extract

Stir together sugar and cornstarch in medium saucepan; gradually add milk and egg yolks, stirring until blended. Cook over medium heat, stirring constantly, until mixture comes to a boil. Boil 1 minute, stirring constantly. Remove from heat; stir in butter and vanilla. Cover; refrigerate several hours or until cold.

Makes about 1⅓ cups filling

Dark Cocoa Glaze

3 tablespoons water

2 tablespoons butter or margarine

3 tablespoons HERSHEY'S® Cocoa

1 cup powdered sugar

½ teaspoon vanilla extract

Heat water and butter in small saucepan over medium heat until mixture comes to a boil; remove from heat. Immediately stir in cocoa. Gradually add powdered sugar and vanilla, beating with whisk until smooth and of desired consistency; cool slightly.

Makes about ¾ cup glaze

NESTLÉ® Very Best Fudge

3 cups granulated sugar

1 can (12 fluid ounces) NESTLÉ® CARNATION® Evaporated Milk

¼ cup (½ stick) butter or margarine

½ teaspoon salt

4 cups miniature marshmallows

4 cups (24 ounces or two 12-ounce packages) NESTLÉ® TOLL HOUSE® Semi-Sweet Chocolate Morsels

1 cup chopped pecans or walnuts (optional)

2 teaspoons vanilla extract

Prep Time: 10 minutes
Cooking Time: 10 minutes
Cooling Time: 2 hours refrigerating

LINE 13×9-inch baking pan or two 8-inch-square baking pans with foil.

COMBINE sugar, evaporated milk, butter and salt in 4- to 5-quart *heavy-duty* saucepan. Bring to a *full rolling boil* over medium heat, stirring constantly. Boil, stirring constantly, for 4 to 5 minutes. Remove from heat.

STIR in marshmallows, morsels, nuts and vanilla extract. Stir vigorously for 1 minute or until marshmallows are melted. Pour into prepared pan(s). Refrigerate for 2 hours or until firm. Lift from pan; remove foil. Cut into pieces. Store tightly covered in refrigerator. Makes about 4 pounds.

Makes 48 servings (2 pieces per serving)

For Milk Chocolate Fudge: SUBSTITUTE 3½ cups (23 ounces) or 2 packages (11.5 ounces *each*) NESTLÉ® TOLL HOUSE® Milk Chocolate Morsels for Semi-Sweet Chocolate Morsels.

For Butterscotch Fudge: SUBSTITUTE 3⅓ cups (22 ounces) or 2 packages (11 ounces *each*) NESTLÉ® TOLL HOUSE® Butterscotch Flavored Morsels for Semi-Sweet Chocolate Morsels.

For Peanutty Fudge: SUBSTITUTE 3⅓ cups (22 ounces) or 2 packages (11 ounces *each*) NESTLÉ® TOLL HOUSE® Peanut Butter & Milk Chocolate Morsels for Semi-Sweet Chocolate Morsels and ½ cup chopped peanuts for pecans or walnuts.

Choco-Berry Cooler

¾ cup cold milk

¼ cup sliced fresh strawberries

2 tablespoons HERSHEY'S® Syrup

2 tablespoons plus 2 small scoops vanilla ice cream, divided

Cold ginger ale or club soda

Fresh strawberry and mint leaves (optional)

1. Place milk, strawberries, chocolate syrup and 2 tablespoons ice cream in blender container. Cover and blend until smooth.

2. Alternate remaining 2 scoops of ice cream and chocolate mixture in tall ice cream soda glass; fill glass with ginger ale. Garnish with a fresh strawberry and mint leaves, if desired. Serve immediately.

Makes 1 (14-ounce) serving

Variations: Before blending, substitute one of the following fruits for fresh strawberries • 3 tablespoons frozen strawberries with syrup, thawed • ½ peeled fresh peach or ⅓ cup canned peach slices • 2 slices canned pineapple or ¼ cup canned crushed pineapple • ¼ cup sweetened fresh raspberries or 3 tablespoons frozen raspberries with syrup, thawed

Chocolate Pecan Pie

1 **cup sugar**

⅓ **cup HERSHEY'S® Cocoa**

3 **eggs, lightly beaten**

¾ **cup light corn syrup**

1 **tablespoon butter or margarine, melted**

1 **teaspoon vanilla extract**

1 **cup pecan halves**

1 **unbaked (9-inch) pie crust**

Whipped topping (optional)

1. Heat oven to 350°F.

2. Stir together sugar and cocoa in medium bowl. Add eggs, corn syrup, butter and vanilla; stir until well blended. Stir in pecans. Pour into unbaked pie crust.

3. Bake 60 minutes or until set. Remove to wire rack; cool completely. Garnish with whipped topping, if desired.

Makes 8 servings

Gimme S'more Pie

1 *prepared* 9-inch (6 ounces) graham cracker crumb crust

1 can (12 fluid ounces) NESTLÉ® CARNATION® Evaporated Milk, *divided*

1 package (3.9 ounces) chocolate instant pudding and pie filling mix

3 cups mini marshmallows, *divided*

2 cups frozen whipped topping, thawed

½ cup NESTLÉ® TOLL HOUSE® Milk Chocolate Morsels

Prep Time: 20 minutes
Cooling Time: 2 hours refrigerating

WHISK *1¼ cups* evaporated milk and pudding mix in medium bowl until well blended. Pour into crust.

MICROWAVE *2 cups* marshmallows and *remaining ¼ cup* evaporated milk in medium, uncovered, microwave-safe bowl on HIGH (100%) power for 30 to 45 seconds; stir until smooth. Let stand for 15 minutes. Gently fold in whipped topping. Spoon marshmallow mixture over chocolate layer; smooth top with spatula.

REFRIGERATE for 2 hours or until set. Top with *remaining 1 cup* marshmallows and morsels.

Makes 8 servings

TIP

For a gooey S'more topping, place chilled pie on a baking sheet. Preheat broiler. Place baking sheet with pie on rack 6 inches from broiler unit (pie top should be at least 4 inches from broiler unit). Broil for 30 seconds or until marshmallows are light brown and morsels are shiny. Watch carefully as browning occurs very fast! A handheld kitchen butane torch can be used as well.

Hot Cocoa Mix

2 cups nonfat dry milk powder

¾ cup sugar

½ cup HERSHEY'S® Cocoa

½ cup powdered non-dairy creamer

Dash salt

Combine all ingredients in large bowl; stir to blend well. Store in tightly covered container.

Makes 3¾ cups mix (about fifteen 6-ounce servings)

Single Serving: Place ¼ cup mix in heatproof cup or mug; add ¾ cup boiling water. Stir to blend. Serve hot, topped with marshmallows, if desired.

Easy As Ice Cream Pie

1 container (1.5 quarts) your favorite BREYERS® All Natural Ice Cream, slightly softened

1 (9-inch) chocolate crumb crust or graham cracker crust

½ to ¾ cup SKIPPY® CREAMY or SUPER CHUNK® Peanut Butter, melted

2 tablespoons chocolate sprinkles

Prep Time: 15 minutes
Freeze Time: 30 minutes

SCOOP BREYERS® All Natural Ice Cream into prepared crust. Drizzle with melted SKIPPY® Creamy Peanut Butter, then add sprinkles. Cover and freeze until ready to serve. Let stand 5 minutes before slicing. Garnish, if desired, with your favorite sundae toppings.

Makes 12 servings

TIP

Try using BREYERS® SMOOTH & DREAMY™ ½ the Fat Ice Cream and SKIPPY® Reduced Fat Creamy Peanut Butter for a special treat!

NESTLÉ® TOLL HOUSE®
Chocolate Chip Cookie Truffles

1 package (16.5 ounces) NESTLÉ® TOLL HOUSE® Refrigerated Chocolate Chip Cookie Bar Dough

1 package (3 ounces) cream cheese, at room temperature

1 cup (6 ounces) NESTLÉ® TOLL HOUSE® Semi-Sweet Chocolate Morsels

1 tablespoon vegetable shortening

1 tablespoon NESTLÉ® TOLL HOUSE® Baking Cocoa, for dusting (optional)

Prep Time: 20 minutes
Cooking Time: 14 minutes

PREHEAT oven to 350°F.

PREPARE cookies following package directions; however, bake for 14 to 18 minutes until crisp and golden brown **but not burnt.** (Crisp cookies will make it easier to grind the cookies later.) Let cookies cool completely on wire racks.

LINE baking sheet with wax paper.

CRUMBLE cookies into food processor container; cover. Process until mixture resembles coarse meal. Add cream cheese; process until mixture begins to hold together. Mixture will be dark in color. (If smaller food processor is being used, half the cookies and half the cream cheese can be processed. Transfer mixture to medium bowl and then repeat with remaining cookies and cream cheese.)

ROLL or scoop mixture into 1-inch balls and place on prepared baking sheet. Refrigerate for 1 hour.

MICROWAVE morsels and vegetable shortening in small, uncovered, microwave-safe bowl on HIGH (100%) power for 1 minute; STIR. Morsels may retain some of their original shape. If necessary, microwave at additional 10- to 15-second intervals, stirring just until morsels are melted.

DIP balls completely into melted chocolate with fork. Use side of bowl or shake gently to remove excess chocolate. Return to baking sheet; dust truffles with cocoa. Refrigerate for 30 minutes or until set. Store in tightly covered container in refrigerator.

Makes 3 dozen candies

Classic Chocolate Cream Pie

5 sections (½ ounce each) HERSHEY'S® Unsweetened Chocolate Baking Bar, broken into pieces

3 cups milk, divided

1⅓ cups sugar

3 tablespoons all-purpose flour

3 tablespoons cornstarch

½ teaspoon salt

3 egg yolks

2 tablespoons butter or margarine

1½ teaspoons vanilla extract

1 baked (9-inch) pie crust, cooled, or 1 (9-inch) crumb crust

Sweetened whipped cream (optional)

1. Combine chocolate and 2 cups milk in medium saucepan; cook over medium heat, stirring constantly, just until mixture boils. Remove from heat and set aside.

2. Stir together sugar, flour, cornstarch and salt in medium bowl. Whisk remaining 1 cup milk into egg yolks in separate bowl; stir into sugar mixture. Gradually add to chocolate mixture. Cook over medium heat, whisking constantly, until mixture boils; boil and stir 1 minute. Remove from heat; stir in butter and vanilla.

3. Pour into prepared crust; press plastic wrap directly onto surface. Cool; refrigerate until well chilled. Top with whipped cream, if desired.

Makes 8 servings

Easy Fruit Parfaits

1 cup boiling water

1 pkg. (4-serving size) gelatin, any red flavor

1 cup cold water

    Frozen nondairy whipped topping, thawed

1 can (15.25 oz.) DOLE® Tropical Fruit, drained

Prep Time: 5 minutes
Chill Time: 4 hours

• Stir boiling water into gelatin in medium bowl 2 minutes until completely dissolved. Stir in cold water. Pour gelatin into 4 tall dessert or parfait glasses, filling about half full.

• Refrigerate 4 hours or until firm. To serve, layer with whipped topping and tropical fruit.

Makes 4 servings

All-Chocolate Boston Cream Pie

1 **cup all-purpose flour**

1 **cup sugar**

⅓ **cup HERSHEY'S® Cocoa**

½ **teaspoon baking soda**

6 **tablespoons butter or margarine, softened**

1 **cup milk**

1 **egg**

1 **teaspoon vanilla extract**

CHOCOLATE FILLING (recipe follows)

SATINY CHOCOLATE GLAZE (recipe follows)

1. Heat oven to 350°F. Grease and flour one 9-inch round baking pan.

2. Stir together flour, sugar, cocoa and baking soda in large bowl. Add butter, milk, egg and vanilla. Beat on low speed of mixer until all ingredients are moistened. Beat on medium speed 2 minutes. Pour batter into prepared pan.

3. Bake 30 to 35 minutes or until wooden pick inserted in center comes out clean. Cool 10 minutes; remove from pan to wire rack. Cool completely. Prepare CHOCOLATE FILLING. Cut cake into two thin layers. Place one layer on serving plate; spread filling over layer. Top with remaining layer.

4. Prepare SATINY CHOCOLATE GLAZE. Pour onto top of cake, allowing some to drizzle down sides. Refrigerate until serving time. Cover; refrigerate leftover cake.

Makes 12 servings

Chocolate Filling

½ **cup sugar**

¼ **cup HERSHEY'S® Cocoa**

2 **tablespoons cornstarch**

1½ **cups light cream**

1 **tablespoon butter or margarine**

1 **teaspoon vanilla extract**

Stir together sugar, cocoa and cornstarch in medium saucepan; gradually stir in light cream. Cook over medium heat, stirring constantly, until mixture thickens and begins to boil. Boil 1 minute, stirring constantly; remove from heat. Stir in butter and vanilla. Press plastic wrap directly onto surface. Cool completely.

Satiny Chocolate Glaze

2 tablespoons water

1 tablespoon butter or margarine

1 tablespoon corn syrup

2 tablespoons HERSHEY'S® Cocoa

¾ cup powdered sugar

½ teaspoon vanilla extract

Heat water, butter and corn syrup in small saucepan to boiling. Remove from heat; immediately stir in cocoa. With whisk, gradually beat in powdered sugar and vanilla until smooth; cool slightly.

Easy NESTLÉ® TOLL HOUSE®
Cookie Fudge

12 squares NESTLÉ® TOLL HOUSE® Refrigerated Chocolate Chip Cookie Bar Dough

2 cups (12-ounce package) NESTLÉ® TOLL HOUSE® Semi-Sweet Chocolate Morsels

1 can (14 ounces) NESTLÉ® CARNATION® Sweetened Condensed Milk

1 teaspoon vanilla extract

Prep Time: 30 minutes
Cooking Time: 10 minutes
Cooling Time: 2 hours refrigerating

PREHEAT oven to 350°F.

BAKE cookies according to package directions. Cool on baking sheet for 2 minutes; remove to wire rack to cool completely. Chop cookies into ½-inch pieces (about 2 cups).

LINE 8-inch-square baking pan with foil.

COMBINE morsels and sweetened condensed milk in medium, *heavy-duty* saucepan. Warm over *lowest possible* heat, stirring until smooth. Remove from heat; stir in *1½ cups* cookie pieces and vanilla extract.

SPREAD evenly into prepared baking pan. Sprinkle with *remaining ½ cup* cookie pieces, pressing in gently. Refrigerate for 2 hours or until firm. Lift from pan; remove foil. Cut into 48 pieces.

Makes 24 servings (2 pieces per serving)

Mini Chocolate Pies

1 **package (4-serving size) vanilla cook & serve pudding and pie filling mix***

1 **cup HERSHEY'S® Mini Chips Semi-Sweet Chocolate**

1 **package (4 ounces) single-serve graham cracker crusts (6 crusts)**

Whipped topping

Additional HERSHEY'S® Mini Chips Semi-Sweet Chocolate, HERSHEY'S® SPECIAL DARK® Chocolate Chips or HERSHEY'S® Semi-Sweet Chocolate Chips (optional)

*Do not use instant pudding mix.

1. Prepare pudding and pie filling mix as directed on package; remove from heat. Immediately add 1 cup small chocolate chips; stir until melted. Cool 5 minutes, stirring occasionally.

2. Pour filling into crusts; press plastic wrap directly onto surface. Refrigerate several hours or until firm. Garnish with whipped topping and small chocolate chips, if desired.

Makes 6 servings

Fudge Brownie Pie

2 eggs

1 cup sugar

½ cup (1 stick) butter or margarine, melted

½ cup all-purpose flour

⅓ cup HERSHEY'S® Cocoa

¼ teaspoon salt

1 teaspoon vanilla extract

½ cup chopped nuts (optional)

Ice cream

HOT FUDGE SAUCE (recipe follows)

1. Heat oven to 350°F. Lightly grease 8-inch pie plate.

2. Beat eggs in medium bowl; blend in sugar and melted butter. Stir together flour, cocoa and salt; add to butter mixture. Stir in vanilla and nuts, if desired. Pour into prepared pie plate.

3. Bake 25 to 30 minutes or until almost set. (Pie will not test done in center.) Cool; cut into wedges. Serve topped with scoop of ice cream and drizzled with HOT FUDGE SAUCE.

Makes 8 servings

Hot Fudge Sauce

¾ cup sugar

½ cup HERSHEY'S® Cocoa

½ cup plus 2 tablespoons (5-ounce can) evaporated milk

⅓ cup light corn syrup

⅓ cup butter or margarine

1 teaspoon vanilla extract

1. Combine sugar and cocoa in medium saucepan; blend in evaporated milk and corn syrup. Cook over medium heat, stirring constantly, until mixture boils; boil and stir 1 minute.

2. Remove from heat; stir in butter and vanilla. Serve warm sauce over ice cream or other desserts.

Makes about 1¾ cups sauce

Microwave Directions: Stir together sugar and cocoa in medium microwave-safe bowl. Gradually add evaporated milk, stirring until blended. Stir in corn syrup. Microwave at HIGH (100%) 1 to 3 minutes, stirring after each minute, until mixture boils. Stir in butter and vanilla. Serve warm.

Mint Fudge Sauce: Add ¼ teaspoon mint extract with the vanilla.

White Chip Fruit Tart

¾ cup (1½ sticks) butter or margarine, softened

½ cup powdered sugar

1½ cups all-purpose flour

2 cups (12-ounce package) HERSHEY'S® Premier White Chips

¼ cup whipping cream

1 package (8 ounces) cream cheese, softened

FRUIT TOPPING (recipe follows)

Assorted fresh fruit, sliced

1. Heat oven to 300°F.

2. Beat butter and powdered sugar in small bowl until smooth; blend in flour. Press mixture onto bottom and up side of 12-inch round pizza pan. Flute edge, if desired.

3. Bake 20 to 25 minutes or until lightly browned; cool completely.

4. Place white chips and whipping cream in medium microwave-safe bowl. Microwave at MEDIUM (50%) 1 to 1½ minutes or until chips are melted and mixture is smooth when stirred. Beat in cream cheese. Spread on cooled crust. Prepare FRUIT TOPPING. Arrange fruit over chip mixture; carefully pour or brush topping over fruit. Cover; refrigerate assembled tart until just before serving.

Makes 10 servings

Fruit Topping

¼ cup sugar

1 tablespoon cornstarch

½ cup pineapple juice

½ teaspoon lemon juice

Stir together sugar and cornstarch in small saucepan; stir in juices. Cook over medium heat, stirring constantly, until thickened; cool.

CARNATION® Famous Fudge

1½ **cups granulated sugar**

⅔ **cup (5 fluid-ounce can) NESTLÉ® CARNATION® Evaporated Milk**

2 **tablespoons butter or margarine**

¼ **teaspoon salt**

2 **cups miniature marshmallows**

1½ **cups (9 ounces) NESTLÉ® TOLL HOUSE® Semi-Sweet Chocolate Morsels**

½ **cup chopped pecans or walnuts (optional)**

1 **teaspoon vanilla extract**

Prep Time: 8 minutes
Cooking Time: 6 minutes
Cooling Time: 2 hours refrigerating

LINE 8-inch-square baking pan with foil.

COMBINE sugar, evaporated milk, butter and salt in medium, *heavy-duty* saucepan. Bring to a *full rolling boil* over medium heat, stirring constantly. Boil, stirring constantly, for 4 to 5 minutes. Remove from heat.

STIR in marshmallows, morsels, nuts and vanilla extract. Stir vigorously for 1 minute or until marshmallows are melted. Pour into prepared baking pan; refrigerate for 2 hours or until firm. Lift from pan; remove foil. Cut into 48 pieces.

Makes 24 servings (2 pieces per serving)

Milk Chocolate Fudge: SUBSTITUTE 1¾ cups (11.5-ounce package) NESTLÉ® TOLL HOUSE® Milk Chocolate Morsels for Semi-Sweet Morsels.

Butterscotch Fudge: SUBSTITUTE 1⅔ cups (11-ounce package) NESTLÉ® TOLL HOUSE® Butterscotch Flavored Morsels for Semi-Sweet Morsels.

Peanutty Chocolate Fudge: SUBSTITUTE 1⅔ cups (11-ounce package) NESTLÉ® TOLL HOUSE® Peanut Butter & Milk Chocolate Morsels for Semi-Sweet Morsels and ½ cup chopped peanuts for pecans or walnuts.

SPECIAL DARK® Fudge Fondue

2 cups (12-ounce package) HERSHEY'S® SPECIAL DARK® Chocolate Chips

½ cup light cream

2 teaspoons vanilla extract

Assorted fondue dippers such as marshmallows, cherries, grapes, mandarin orange segments, pineapple chunks, strawberries, slices of other fresh fruits, small pieces of cake or small brownies

1. Place chocolate chips and light cream in medium microwave-safe bowl. Microwave at MEDIUM (50%) 1 minute or just until chips are melted and mixture is smooth when stirred. Stir in vanilla.

2. Pour into fondue pot or chafing dish; serve warm with fondue dippers. If mixture thickens, stir in additional light cream, 1 tablespoon at a time. Refrigerate leftover fondue.

Makes 1½ cups

Stovetop Directions: Combine chocolate chips and light cream in heavy medium saucepan. Cook over low heat, stirring constantly, until chips are melted and mixture is hot. Stir in vanilla and continue as in Step 2 above.

NESTLÉ® TOLL HOUSE®
Chocolate Chip Pie

1 *unbaked* 9-inch (4-cup volume) deep-dish pie shell*

2 large eggs

½ cup all-purpose flour

½ cup granulated sugar

½ cup packed brown sugar

¾ cup (1½ sticks) butter, softened

1 cup (6 ounces) NESTLÉ® TOLL HOUSE® Semi-Sweet Chocolate Morsels

1 cup chopped nuts

Sweetened whipped cream or ice cream (optional)

*If using frozen pie shell, use deep-dish style, thawed completely. Bake on baking sheet; increase baking time slightly.

Prep Time: 15 minutes
Baking Time: 55 minutes
Cooling Time: 15 minutes

PREHEAT oven to 325°F.

BEAT eggs in large mixer bowl on high speed until foamy. Beat in flour, granulated sugar and brown sugar. Beat in butter. Stir in morsels and nuts. Spoon into pie shell.

BAKE for 55 to 60 minutes or until knife inserted halfway between outside edge and center comes out clean. Cool on wire rack. Serve warm with whipped cream, if desired.

Makes 8 servings

Mini LIBBY'S® Famous Pumpkin Pies

- **4 (1-cup volume *each*) 4-inch diameter mini-pie shells**
- **¾ cup granulated sugar**
- **1 teaspoon ground cinnamon**
- **½ teaspoon salt**
- **½ teaspoon ground ginger**
- **¼ teaspoon ground cloves**
- **2 large eggs**
- **1 can (15 ounces) LIBBY'S® 100% Pure Pumpkin**
- **1 can (12 fluid ounces) NESTLÉ® CARNATION® Evaporated Milk**

Prep Time: 8 minutes
Baking Time: 45 minutes
Cooling Time: 2 hours

PREHEAT oven to 425°F.

MIX sugar, cinnamon, salt, ginger and cloves in small bowl. Beat eggs lightly in large bowl. Stir in pumpkin and sugar-spice mixture. Gradually stir in evaporated milk.

POUR into shells.

BAKE for 15 minutes. Reduce oven temperature to 350°F. Bake for 30 to 35 minutes or until knife inserted near center comes out clean. Cool on wire rack for 2 hours. Serve immediately or refrigerate. (Do not freeze as this may cause filling to separate from the crust.)

Makes 4 mini pies

Note: May use refrigerated or homemade single pie crust to make 4 mini-pie shells. Lay rim of mini-pie pan on rolled out dough. Cut circle ½ inch larger than mini-pie pan to allow for dough to form fluted edge.

Lower Fat & Calorie Pies: Substitute NESTLÉ® CARNATION® Lowfat Evaporated or Fat Free Evaporated Milk.

HERSHEY'S® Rich Cocoa Fudge

3 cups sugar

⅔ cup HERSHEY'S® Cocoa
   or HERSHEY'S® SPECIAL
   DARK® Cocoa

⅛ teaspoon salt

1½ cups milk

¼ cup (½ stick) butter

1 teaspoon vanilla extract

1. Line 8- or 9-inch square pan with foil, extending foil over edges of pan. Butter foil.

2. Stir together sugar, cocoa and salt in heavy 4-quart saucepan; stir in milk. Cook over medium heat, stirring constantly, until mixture comes to full rolling boil. Boil, without stirring, until mixture reaches 234°F on candy thermometer or until small amount of mixture dropped into very cold water forms a soft ball which flattens when removed from water. (Bulb of candy thermometer should not rest on bottom of saucepan.) Remove from heat.

3. Add butter and vanilla. DO NOT STIR. Cool at room temperature to 110°F (lukewarm). Beat with wooden spoon until fudge thickens and just begins to lose some of its gloss. Quickly spread in prepared pan; cool completely. Cut into squares. Store in tightly covered container at room temperature.

Makes about 3 dozen pieces or 1¾ pounds candy

Nutty Rich Cocoa Fudge: Beat cooked fudge as directed. Immediately stir in 1 cup chopped almonds, pecans or walnuts and quickly spread in prepared pan.

Marshmallow Nut Cocoa Fudge: Increase cocoa to ¾ cup. Cook fudge as directed. Add 1 cup marshmallow creme with butter and vanilla. DO NOT STIR. Cool to 110°F (lukewarm). Beat 8 minutes; stir in 1 cup chopped nuts. Pour into prepared pan. (Fudge does not set until poured into pan.)

Notes:
For best results, do not double this recipe.

This is one of our most requested recipes, but also one of our most difficult. The directions must be followed exactly. Beat too little and the fudge is too soft. Beat too long and it becomes hard and sugary.

Index

Acknowledgments

The publisher would like to thank the companies and organizations below for the use of their recipes and photographs in this publication.

The Beef Checkoff

Butterball® Turkey

Campbell Soup Company

Cream of Wheat Cereal,
A Division of B&G Foods
North America, Inc.

Del Monte Foods

Dole Food Company, Inc.

Equal® 0 Calorie Sweetener

Heinz North America

The Hershey Company

Hormel Foods. LLC

Jennie-O Turkey Store, LLC

®Johnsonville Sausage, LLC

Nestlé USA

Ortega®, A Division of B&G
Foods North America, Inc.

The Quaker® Oatmeal Kitchens

Reckitt Benckiser LLC

Sargento® Foods Inc.

StarKist®

© 2010 Sunbean Products, Inc.
doing business as Jarden
Consumer Solutions.

Sunkist Growers Inc.

Unilever

Metric Conversion Chart

VOLUME MEASUREMENTS (dry)

$1/8$ teaspoon = 0.5 mL
$1/4$ teaspoon = 1 mL
$1/2$ teaspoon = 2 mL
$3/4$ teaspoon = 4 mL
1 teaspoon = 5 mL
1 tablespoon = 15 mL
2 tablespoons = 30 mL
$1/4$ cup = 60 mL
$1/3$ cup = 75 mL
$1/2$ cup = 125 mL
$2/3$ cup = 150 mL
$3/4$ cup = 175 mL
1 cup = 250 mL
2 cups = 1 pint = 500 mL
3 cups = 750 mL
4 cups = 1 quart = 1 L

VOLUME MEASUREMENTS (fluid)

1 fluid ounce (2 tablespoons) = 30 mL
4 fluid ounces ($1/2$ cup) = 125 mL
8 fluid ounces (1 cup) = 250 mL
12 fluid ounces ($1 1/2$ cups) = 375 mL
16 fluid ounces (2 cups) = 500 mL

WEIGHTS (mass)

$1/2$ ounce = 15 g
1 ounce = 30 g
3 ounces = 90 g
4 ounces = 120 g
8 ounces = 225 g
10 ounces = 285 g
12 ounces = 360 g
16 ounces = 1 pound = 450 g

DIMENSIONS

$1/16$ inch = 2 mm
$1/8$ inch = 3 mm
$1/4$ inch = 6 mm
$1/2$ inch = 1.5 cm
$3/4$ inch = 2 cm
1 inch = 2.5 cm

OVEN TEMPERATURES

250°F = 120°C
275°F = 140°C
300°F = 150°C
325°F = 160°C
350°F = 180°C
375°F = 190°C
400°F = 200°C
425°F = 220°C
450°F = 230°C

BAKING PAN SIZES

Utensil	Size in Inches/Quarts	Metric Volume	Size in Centimeters
Baking or Cake Pan (square or rectangular)	$8 \times 8 \times 2$	2 L	$20 \times 20 \times 5$
	$9 \times 9 \times 2$	2.5 L	$23 \times 23 \times 5$
	$12 \times 8 \times 2$	3 L	$30 \times 20 \times 5$
	$13 \times 9 \times 2$	3.5 L	$33 \times 23 \times 5$
Loaf Pan	$8 \times 4 \times 3$	1.5 L	$20 \times 10 \times 7$
	$9 \times 5 \times 3$	2 L	$23 \times 13 \times 7$
Round Layer Cake Pan	$8 \times 1 1/2$	1.2 L	20×4
	$9 \times 1 1/2$	1.5 L	23×4
Pie Plate	$8 \times 1 1/4$	750 mL	20×3
	$9 \times 1 1/4$	1 L	23×3
Baking Dish or Casserole	1 quart	1 L	—
	$1 1/2$ quarts	1.5 L	—
	2 quarts	2 L	—